after words

ESSENTIAL POETS SERIES 213

**Canada Council
for the Arts**

**Conseil des Arts
du Canada**

Guernica Editions Inc. acknowledges
the support of the Canada Council
for the Arts and the Ontario Arts Council.
The Ontario Arts Council
is an agency of the Government
of Ontario.

We acknowledge the financial support of the
Government of Canada through the Canada
Book Fund (CBF) for our publishing activities.

**ONTARIO ARTS COUNCIL
CONSEIL DES ARTS DE L'ONTARIO**

50 YEARS OF ONTARIO GOVERNMENT SUPPORT OF THE ARTS
50 ANS DE SOUTIEN DU GOUVERNEMENT DE L'ONTARIO AUX ARTS

STAN ROGAL

after words

GUERNICA

TORONTO – BUFFALO – LANCASTER (U.K.)
2014

Michael Mirolla, editor
Guernica Editions Inc.
P.O. Box 76080, Abbey Market, Oakville, (ON), Canada L6M 3H5
2250 Military Road, Tonawanda, N.Y. 14150-6000 U.S.A.

Distributors:
University of Toronto Press Distribution,
5201 Dufferin Street, Toronto (ON), Canada M3H 5T8
Gazelle Book Services, White Cross Mills, High Town, Lancaster LA1 4XS U.K.

First edition.
Printed in Canada.

Legal Deposit – Third Quarter
Library of Congress Catalog Card Number: 2014934786
Library and Archives Canada Cataloguing in Publication

Rogal, Stan, 1950-, author
After words / Stan Rogal.

(Essential poets series ; 213)
Poems.
Issued in print and electronic formats.
ISBN 978-1-55071-861-4 (pbk.).--ISBN 978-1-55071-862-1 (epub).--
ISBN 978-1-55071-863-8 (mobi)

I. Title. II. Series: Essential poets series ; 213

PS8585.O391A37 2014   C811'.54   C2014-900220-3
                                                C2014-900221-1

*To Marja Moens and Heather Cadsby, who told me
I'd discovered "the chink in the armour"
when they decided to publish my first collection of poetry
with Wolsak and Wynn, way back when – many thanks!*

■ Contents

When I begin to write after a rather long interval,
I draw the words as if out of the empty air.
If I capture one, then I have just this one alone
and all the toil must begin anew.
— Franz Kafka

The poem of the mind
and the act of finding what will suffice.
— Wallace Stevens

After the novels, after the teacups, after the skirts
that trail along the floor.
After this, and so much more?
It is impossible to say just what I mean!
— T.S. Eliot

MILTON ACORN

I'll be honest, I shied away from the poetry of Milton Acorn for the longest time. Why? Because my only association with either him or his work was through the titular "People's Poet/ ry" movement and its gamut of contests and anthologies which served to produce what I thought was some of the worst poetry ever written: trite, clichéd, simplistic, flat, sentimental, boring and usually (actually) prose broken into short lines on a page so as to resemble a poem (not all, of course, cream rises and so on, and me not wanting to paint the entire picture with a single wide bleak brush, though …)

To each their own and one person's junk is another's treasure, yes, but … really … I didn't (don't) get it.

Taking a poetry course at York University I was introduced to the work and life of Gwendolyn MacEwen and her tumultuous affair/relationship/marriage with a certain Milton Acorn and I thought – crazy! What a wild mad disturbed pair. And she loved him first and foremost for his poetry. Maybe it was time to check out the bastard and see what the appeal was.

What I discovered was a poet who had set the bar high; whose inner voice was powerful and whose study and range was vast and deep – *I've tasted my own blood* – a line from Arthur Rimbaud. Say no more.

He left shoes that are tough to fill by any so-called "People's Poet".

Island

after Milton Acorn

"I worry about the shape of my skull"

Grimly outlined by the salt squall
in such grey matter it hung
uncertain
to the finish, as:
                    what might come of it?

Here, &, alive at the margins (barely)
    the famous writer, pensive, now stops & lights a cigar.

Delivered on a plate to a vengeful Salome?
Split apart by wisdom's leggy kick?
Gone to line mackinaw men with a fine-combed tooth?
No carpenter with a cross to bear
could drive the nail
so deep as this beerfog boy
nor cause such unholy stir
    that shivered timbers of Trotskyites & Snarks the same.
Who had been known to give skull to a minor
took serious to heart.
Boldfaced, fer sure, brass-balled & backwoodsy
    with a sprawl of crags, crevasses &
        thick underbrush ghosted down for the count.
Boo!
Call him Ishmael. Call him Shadow-maker.
Who'd've sparked a fine grave roller if provisioned a
    rat's ass

chance, instead, was bushwhacked; cut off at the neck
& made a bust.
Through no fault, save, to preserve a mean reputation,
meaning, apart the common red dirt that conjures
   an island
from this twisted wreckage

               (say: *pee-eye*, say: *spud*, say: *Minago*)

sprung a low brow cast of dead fish; so-called people's
   poets
with little taste for blood – their own or any other reckless
spill, &
    beyond the uneasy drift of smoke & ash from the
  vacant socket
       pronounced a breed of missionary position
         set to bugger waters generations to follow
with their thin colourless milt.

ANTONIN ARTAUD

Speaking of crazy, mad bastards – actor/playwright Antonin Artaud ended in an asylum for the insane and died from cancer of the bunghole, apparently one of the most painful types of cancers anyone can suffer through. His one written play was titled *Spurt of Blood* and was a mere five minutes long. He spent years attempting to produce *Les Cenci* in a manner that would break down the barriers between audience and actors and was vilified from all directions. Unbelievably handsome in his youth, he soon wasted away due to drugs and sickness (think Chet Baker).

Any wonder why he called his theatre the "Theatre of Cruelty"?

He attempted to create works that depended less on text and more on the visceral and emotive aspects of live theatre. He ultimately failed, BUT … it was a grand failure.

What I attempt to do with this monologue is to fill the stage with a busted narrative that depends more on imagery than provide a linear meaning while at the same time have the actor perform actions that have little or nothing to do with the text – ear and eye candy to be assimilated and deciphered by the brain and heart of each individual audience member.

Theatre Of Cruelty: Audition Piece

after Antonin Artaud

"No more masterpieces"

A young soldier stands in a halo of light and speaks to the audience. It's as if he's looking in a mirror. As he speaks, he undresses, folds his uniform and stacks it neatly on the floor in front of him alongside his rifle, knife and duffle bag.

The dry heaves choke ghosts from my throat. Gutting to the feathers. When the bough breaks there are no cogs, wheels or rubber belts. No berries for a pie. No Cracker Jack's prize. A penny whistle. The moon sucks black with smoke. The sun is blind. Pictures worth a thousand words. Where is that slack-jawed music? Clementine. I named my dog Beethoven and played the zither. A skinned rabbit collects flies. When the head drops off, eat it. The naked dead. Know your arm from your elbow, your ass from a hole in the ground. My arms are knives. Lice tap-dance in my armpits. Climb up on my shoulders, son. A parade of skeletons. Lemonade on a hot afternoon. Buttered corn. Barbed wire yanked through the liver. A knife in the heart. A bucket of tears. Alone in a rocker. Fingernails across a blackboard. The dull shiver of infantry. Gooseflesh on my tongue. My hand in the lawnmower. This is your rifle, this is your gun, one is for killing, the other for fun. My feet sink in bombed ground. The idle chatter of machine guns. Echoes of a boxed lunch. Halos of fireflies. Hellos and goodbyes. Wipe my ass with a bayonet. Move your butt soldier. My head in the latrine. The old swimming hole. Foaming with piss. Choking in mud. If it moves, shoot it. Run for my life. (*Gives a quick glance over the shoulder.*) A picnic at the beach. (*Turns back to the audience.*) Mom and dad holding hands. A brand new mitt. Shitting my pants. A bullet in the head. A murder of crows. A blaze of rape seed. A freeze of oranges. A bloodied nose. Don't cry. Don't cry. The hollow voice of God. A death in the family. Where do clouds go? What does nothing look like? The sharp light of reason. The drum of artillery. Halloween kisses. Spinners. Sparklers. Roman candles. Tiger bombs. Baby fingers. Ohs, oohs and ahs. Screams. Cries. Howls. Whispers. Murmurs. Laments. The riotous dead. Jesus, he was a handsome man. Meat curing in a window. Hot dogs on a barbecue. Poppies on a carcass. Smacking ketchup from the bottle. Flowers crushing beneath boots. A clench of daffodils. A disease of carnations. A stench of roses. The vomit of fried hair. Murder in the cathedral. My brain is mud. There's a bone in my throat. No rest for the wicked. Police in pursuit. Cocks stiff in a row. Mom's homemade jam. Shit on my eyelashes. Egg on my face. A chick with no head. A pair of white tits. Dreaming of salt. The dead never rise. A doughnut for a chest. A head of blonde hair. Cum on my tongue. Oh, my darling. Honeypie. Sugarloaf. Sweetheart. Loverbabe. Pussycat. Cunt. Shoot first, ask questions never. The name of the game. My balls in a vice. The square of the hypotenuse. You can't live on love. Take it like a man. Fuck a snake in a woodpile. Shores washed in moonlight. Loving you madly. A song in my heart. Hell in a handbag. They are not men they are the enemy. Kill or be killed. Don't look back. Matchstick eyes. A fist of snot. A smudge of lemons. A choir of angels. Kill and kill. Hunger of jackhammers. Poisoning the waters. Women and children first. My prick in a beehive. Glory, glory. There's a fly in my soup. Put some of the old pepper on it son. When I grow up I'm gonna be a ball player. Yellow bellied sonofabitch. Gutless bastard. Cowboys and injuns. Stealing scalps from a waistband. Crushing skulls with a rifle butt. Wrapping bodies in flags. (*He gives another quick glance behind.*) Shooting fish in a barrel. (*Turns back to the audience.*) Kill and kill. Dressing the bird. Browning the skin. Eatin' the cracklin'. Reaming my dick. Sucking blood from a nipple. Momma, poppa. Momma, poppa. Blown ass over teakettle. An eye in the ointment. Kill and kill. Rosemary for remembrance. Salt on the radishes. Spit on the sights. Fodder for the cannons. I am nailed to a cross. Safe in my mother's lovin' arms. Kill and kill. This little piggy. A brand on my brain. A thorn in my foot. Chancres eat my genitals. Snipers crouch in every shadow. The puke of green History dribbles my chin. The king is dead. The emperor has no clothes. Kill and kill. (*He is completely naked. He dusts his body in talcum powder. He takes a pair of pajamas out of his duffle bag and proceeds to slip into them.*) Death waits for no man. (*Ponders this last statement, one leg in his pajamas.*) Is this the end of Ricco? (*Pause, then picks up his knife, holds it to his throat, makes a swipe across.*) Spurt of blood. (*He returns the knife to the pile and keeps dressing. He recites very quickly, as if a drill.*) Spiders of light. Rock of ages. Lest we forget. The sins of the fathers. Forgive and forget. The spirit is willing. A flea in her ear. Pi-R-squared. I give you the boy. The meek shall inherent. Together we stand. An apple a day. Step on a crack. Fools rush in. A bird in the hand. A stitch in time. Let him without sin. Cross your heart. Love is a many. To market, to market. Casting pearls. Haste makes. Idle hands. Don't cry. Make hay. Look on. Shape up. Let a. Smile and. Call the. (*Pause as he stands in his pajamas.*) Momma? Poppa? Your son is home. (*The boy gathers his belongings and slips his rifle over his shoulder. He squints ahead. He uses a hand to brush at his hair.*) I'm beat. It's been a long trip to get here. I have to get some sleep. (*He produces a revolver from somewhere, sticks the barrel in his mouth, pulls the trigger. There's an explosion and lights go out. A flash of red, then darkness.*)

MARGARET ATWOOD

I was at York University (years ago) working on my MA. I was taking a Canadian poetry class with Frank Davey and there was a young woman sitting beside me (and when I say 'young' I mean very young as I was there as a mature student and she had plans to have her MA by age 23 and her PhD by age 25 and tenure as a professor by … whatever) who suddenly said something like 'pulling men out of the air and eating them'. I stopped and looked at her and she said, good, finally, I got your attention. I tried all the niceties and was ignored so figured I'd try a line from Margaret Atwood.

We talked some more and she said that generally women prefer Atwood's novels and men prefer her poetry. I tended to agree, though I hadn't read a lot of Atwood's poetry and figured I should take a closer look.

I guess what struck me strongest was that, in the novels, the women tended to be passive/submissive/distant, whereas in the poems, they were more often active/aggressive/present, so, yeah, I did prefer the poems to the novels. There's also more humour in the poems – dry, mischievous, subtle humour, true – which I liked. Of course, in terms of sex, there was always this struggle or war between the sexes and actual intercourse required great mental energy and/or anguish, especially in terms of moving past the politics.

I went with the Shakespearian notion that perhaps "the lady doth protest too much" to explore this struggle and also have some fun.

Circa 1970

after Margaret Atwood

"The body buries itself"

Methinks the lady doth protest too much, tho,
hard pressed to venture who's who in this punished space.
Whether Susanna taken down river, her lean yard cordoned,
her now inviolate carcass a'buzz with the violet pulse of
skeeters, black flies, *no-see-ums*
noumenal glow canted toward
    no art
        no song
            no asylum
                no taste of tea & oranges
merely an institution set to cough in its dead
at the least suspicion: cholera, tuberculosis, paranoid
schizophrenia
orgasm
    any similar melancholic deemed hysteric
for the time.

Or perhaps some further itinerant hobbled
mad as a March *guerre* that ate at wood too sparse
to call a forest.
Who waxed a lonely figure herself
marked a duplicate X in the frosted field
laid out as she was in traditional garb:
    hair shirt
        shaved head
            gooseflesh anointed with ashes
            feet bound in chicken wire & doused in kerosene

mea culpa, mea culpa, mea culpa …
What might normal be considered country matters
goes bats in this fresh wilderness, revolts the brainpan &
    (her favoured sex having no place in this rough bush, seems)
turns tale, seeks transformation toward the other
all the while forgot
                one can never fully be aware
                the exact moment skin barks, fleece constricts
                & horns cut deep into the skull, set, as ever, to grind
a moody girl to rapture
even as the first shovel threatens to fill the hole.

Heady

after Margaret Atwood

"You'll notice that what they have in common
is between their legs"

More 'Exhibit A' than an exhibition, remarks:
   ... turned upside down, they all look the same ...
A penny whistle, perhaps, perhaps
a blunt cigar, rum-dipped, wine-tipped,
perhaps a clothes peg, functional & efficient

                  it teases the ear, the lips
                  the fingers
                  is taken in hand
                  to hang
                  a snatch
                  of moistness
                  on a line

not your moistness; not your line
its tinny music blows blue in the face
reeks of bar stools & the salt taste of empty
intercourse
you take it in your mouth & are almost gentle
hush, you say, *not a word; not a sound;*
not one false move
it never listens
it would hunt you down, except,
    you've erased your scent, again;
        slipped into the skin of some other
Madame X

armoured as ever to haggle situationlessness
among power politics grown two-headed
& lashed one tongue against the other
at any rate, no real wonder as
   … *a hard man being good to find* …
appears out of the question
in this tight space

what might otherwise be termed a joke
if it all wasn't taken so goddamned serious
pins *Peg-o-my-heart* to the sleeve of
eaches vagrant tune smoking wraith-like
from between the legs.

JOHN BARLOW

John was living on Bathurst Street sharing a third-floor apartment with Bill Kennedy. There was a party going on and the apartment had access to the roof. Darren Wershler-Henry was in the kitchen drinking Irish Whiskey and deriding The Eagles and whatever their so-called influence might be on any present-day worthwhile edgy artist or band. Bill was sucking back a beer, pushing back his hair and holding court among a gaggle of earnest young poets. John was outside nodding on a joint, a beer, *yup, yup,* big goofy grin on his face. Peter McPhee was in the middle of a long, long funny story told to someone about something.

Jay MillAr, Angela Rawlings, Sandra Alland, Stephen Cain, Natalee Caple, Christian Bök, Alana Wilcox, Michael Holmes, Stuart Ross … the future of CanLit huddled together in a reek of canned music, booze and potato chips.

I was wandering 'lonely as a cloud' drinking a glass of red wine, leaning over the rail-less roof, soaking up the mixed scene in tattered bits and pieces.

The cats were a'prowl, *meow!*

Gate Crasher

after John Barlow

"A party in which all were not only naked
but amazed and at ease with being so"

What may or may not be a Hitchcockian dream sequence
situates him vertigo at the roof edge, fickle finger of fate to
one side, stars a'twitter on the other, configuring quite divested
Mercury in retrograde, sun in Cancer, moon in Uranus
other constellations unkimonoed vacuously in the swirl
lesser heavenly bodies toppled bare from the bell tower
even Erato defenestrated by the vision of a black habit
that would itself drop naked at the feet of a well-hung corpse
if given a snowball's chance in hell
meanwhile, jammed stalwart on the eave, beer in hand
head ticked with dope, cigarette nailed to lower lip
around him & everywhere neighbouring cats prop like bicycles
against dormer walls, rub fur into cedar shakes & burst into flame
OK, nothing so far out of joint, it seems, him conjecturing
just another Saturday night in the hood when suddenly

       D
           O
               W
                   N

he goes Alice, tumbles arse over tea kettle, sails into
   the firmament
through an open window, stumbles into a room of dead people
who bear resemblances beyond death, say: Moose Lodge, Elk
Royal Order of Buffalo, Legionnaire or Ku Klux Klan members

they initially appear full of merriment, high jinks & shenanigans
they wear funny hats, wave flags, have name tags pinned to lapels
they brandish shots of Jack, mugs of dark ale, tumblers of rye
they puff on fat, hand-rolled Cuban cigars, there are bowls of
potato chips, dip, fake flickering candles laid upon paper
tablecloths
from the kitchen wafts the distinct aromas of baked potatoes
fried steaks & onions, mom's special home-made apple pie
they are surrounded by a bevy of buxom broads clad in classic
spiked heels, lace g-strings, tasselled bras, bouffant hairdos
they sing the same old songs & seem happy enough wearing
each other's faces
nothing politic. bereft of any solid language save secret hand
signs
& unsafe telepathy
they are really living it up!
trouserless, they rush blindly through the blue smoke din
transporting their Beardsley erections in slings, hand carts &
wheelbarrows
their harried chests pounding wet & breathy from the chase
their necks hung with sausage links of coloured condoms
their noses to the wheel, their eyes on the game
doing their best to ignore him (I mean, the joint barely O's)
as if he were an uninvited ghost
it was obvious he reminded them of something best forgotten
maybe:

    the wife, the kids, the family pet
    the job in the office, the warehouse, the factory
    the mortgage on the house, the cottage, the car
    the monthly bills, the insurance policies, the college fund
    the mail taken in, the garbage taken out

he was the hot water tap left running, the back burner left on
he was the not-so-buried memory of middle-class
    North American

guilt complex & the luggage that entailed
he was the bungled opportunity, the ship that never came in
the horse that never finished, the number that never came up
he was the mysterious stranger who augured eternal bliss
& never showed
he was the dreaded three in the morning bad news phone call
he was a stitch in the side, a cold in the nose, an ache in the
head
a stab in the back, a kick in the groin, a bad smell, a rude
noise
a king-sized pain in the ass & a real fucking downer
he was the fly in the ointment, the sty in the eye, the pig in
the poke
the thorn in the rose, the chaff in the wheat, the swine among
pearls
he was the single sour lemon in a field of sweet oranges
he was the thought police, he was *that guy, that guy, you know?*
he was your worst nightmare
he was the missed period that took your youth your dreams
your life
he was HAL

> *"I can tell from your voice harmonics, Dave, that you're
> badly upset."*

damn rights
this due to fear &/or obligation; mostly fear; primarily fear; fear
he was the dangerous alien & not about to spoil the party
the dead turned & doubled in serious laughter, locked arms,
pressed
shoulder to shoulder, forced him out the window & shut the pane
it was then he noticed he too was naked, & amazed & at ease,
&
aw shucks, ma'am, not so bad, this set adrift like a kite floated
toward
the clouds, party noise still ringing his ears: heavy sigh of

ectoplasm
squeals of pinched bottoms, calls for more drinks, growing, raucous
chorus of "John B's Body" raising him above the rooftops into the night air.

DJUNA BARNES

Another book stumbled upon in a used bookstore, what immediately drew my attention/interest to *Nightwood* was the lengthy flattering introduction by T.S. Eliot – holy shit! – and who was this writer and what was this novel to deserve such attention?

I read it and was fascinated. Yes, Paris in the wild nineteen thirties, lesbian lovers and cross-dressing doctors, though the real appeal was the language: intelligent poetic prose without the affectation generally associated with such a description; clean and cutting: "There is not one of us who, given an eternal incognito, a thumbprint nowhere set against our souls, would not commit rape, murder and all abominations. For if pigeons flew out of his bum, or castles sprang out of his ears, man would be troubled to know which was his fate, a house a bird or a man."

With a life at least as *avant-garde* as her novel, I tried to blend the two realms – fiction/fact – within a literary context in this prose poem.

Go Down, Matthew

after Djuna Barnes

"A cut rose, a dead polytechnician; what could be sadder?"

Asked again in demotic French admits something of the bent intercourse, *ooh-la-la!* Vomiting up the last raspberry, yes? Which invokes Céline's journey to night's end without a pot to piss in. Which invokes Eliot's whispered immortality eyed with daffodil bulbs instead of balls. Which invokes Shakespeare's flights of angels rooting in the nunnery. Which invokes myriad further hysteric spooks & unholy ghostlies disguised in widow's weeds stood lip-locked at the watery edge.

All them damned metaphors.

Ophelia a moist flower laid upon the river's bed. Polonius taken from behind the arras.

What were once called graven images. Whether three grasses, nine mouses or twelve apostrophes fails to nail down. As suckled at the ancient breast – Thalia, say, (charged with comic, bucolic poetry & all matters country) – cannot escape the *soi disant* of trousers & inky cloak amid the gush; the gash.

Neverminding a tax collector's dog-eared style bowed over the sermon's mount. Or wigged-out doctor dressed to lie beside himself in a woman's flannel nightgown, pained with wood that strains the painted night's fabric. Or Dante's channelling Mary Baker Eddy from the gates of hell with: *Love insists the loved loves back* & met with some bankrupt line meant to keep a christian soul at heel.

Or this other love's Fool, spurred to the middle of life's trek & discovered herself a lonely rider within the elmèd wood, the straight way lost, the infernal dark river choked with exquisite corpses, empty whiskey bottles, shredded pages of the Ladies Almanack, butt ends of cigarettes who with heavy heart drags her belly along the gutter fills her mouth with rose petals goes down

JOHN BERRYMAN

I confess, my copy of *77 Dream Songs* is split severally at the spine and held together by masking tape and an elastic band, that's how worn it is from reading and re-reading. Of course, I've since purchased his collected works but there's something about flipping through the dog-eared original that takes me back to those early days of discovery: what a powerful and haunting/haunted voice! And am I hard-wired to be attracted to suicides and generally tragic figures (there are more ahead) or is it simple coincidence?

Labelled by history as a key figure among the 'confessional poets' he stood the genre on its head by interrupting the straight narrative form with political/social/literary asides, mixed discourses, alter egos, ribald humour and unapologetic erudition.

All of this together with a lust for life that belied his fated leap from the Washington Avenue bridge in Minneapolis, Minnesota, where he missed the targeted river, landed hard on the west bank and took five days to die.

One Mississippi, two Mississippi, three Mississippi …

Delusions *Etc*

after John Berryman

"literature bores me, especially great literature"

How many years, O, since Henry
huff his lank frame 'cross the wide ocean
to venture out some tale (or, more precise) some
piece o' tale 'pon which to thrust his reaction'ry
erections; his gripes & rails, to spur home
his jaundiced bear to a mean locomotion?

How many, order to claim spurned lover, rejected heart,
unsuited suitor heaved bed to bedlam in the whiskeyed throes?
Her he remembers as (alongside beer & sausage)
Germanic, tho', nothing formal here as idiom drops
among spare change in the furthest corner pockets
& all type fond record is held hostage.

Strange currency, his little books, of sudden, sell
& how is this mischief if not short of miraculous?
& what it was or is that made the words tell?
& who whispered the ear with the wherewithal?
Confused?
The image ghosts of moonlight snatched in blues.

Henry's Lament

after John Berryman

"Fear. Of failure, or, worse, *insignificance*"

O, there are horribles, yes, a'plenty.
Blessings, too, tho' necessarily fewer.
But fame? It would slit our throats to keep us.
Surely. Witness the cover snap of *Time*.
Henry feigned the beard & was struck, aw, by the act
eyes shot red as the assholes of two diarrhetic seagulls.

      They rumour he plucked a nose hair to sing the bawl.

& what of the naked wrest with the dancing bear?
& what of the rangy co-ed he threw a fuck into
with all proper heads turned to heaven?
Or was that another *actual*, heaving; heaved?
Full pregnant with pause was spent before he came.
He re-reads Lear & follies himself mad.
Given over to the drudge of self-perpetuation
he genuflects; nails his peter to the rood.
Look! There is & there isn't a finger
                where a finger shouldn't be.

High on the hog, they quired of him even as
traitorous words exhibited his books as corpses.
Prized him with long cloaks & adrenalin.
Stuck his wings with cigarette butts.
Still. Who cut in & was cut in on shook
his bloody-mindedness beside the weal,
one foot in the confessional, the other in the grave.

An oddity born to sweat delirious the white hotel.
& what remains at close? A vomit of stars.
Riddled daddy a goner. Fame a fleeted thing.
Suicide bird a pretty flap atop the fated bridge.
Past this reckons simply: each dog has its day
Henry hound howls.
Howled.

HUMPHREY BOGART

Growing up, I heard many people comment on the physical resemblance between my dad and Humphrey Bogart. And it was true. I mean, my dad was taller (who wasn't, Bogey being only about five foot eight inches in his shoes and socks.) Beyond that, though, there was the high forehead, the slicked back black hair, the devil-may-care attitude, the whiskey shot and the ever-present cigarette nailed to the lower lip. Plus my dad wore a hat, tipped *a la* Philip Marlowe, that threatened: "When you're slapped, you'll take it and like it."

A tough guy who was also a hit with the ladies. That was my dad.

I mean, that was Bogey.

Rick's American Café

after Humphrey Bogart

What other angered bird man reached such heights
From so much down at heel
Or natural cast a blank eye above the pall
To register full-grown male tease?
Not necessarily home free with the big art
Still
Weathers the storm
Either drunk & disoriented on high sea's era
Or adrift in the holy wood
Casts a wide blanket
Collars each chain-smoking ancient that lisps yours, mine, ours
Among the sin tax
Bacchanal lowering even as the Amazon queen
Leeches homeward on the back log
Catering burn and half-burn where the forest yawled
Hard, bleak, uninhabited though naturally engendered
By a hay seed's ear that air-mailed ease of fallen coin neatly
Feathered
In the mellow drama, dialogue a bust, lurid patter turned to ash
This gin joint out of tune with the mumble of sexual ambiguity
        played again, & again, & again …

RICHARD BRAUTIGAN

I was on holiday with my first wife, driving down the west coast through San Francisco on our way to somewhere further south, we didn't know where, exactly. We were in a used bookstore in the Haight-Ashbury district and she pulled a collection of poems from off a shelf and started flipping through it. She smiled and chuckled and came over and read to me, "I Feel Horrible. She Doesn't" and laughed. I like these. They're funny. And short. And sexy. And I can understand them. Like most of us, she had been raised on long, deadly serious poetry replete with dense allusion, metaphorical significance and vague euphemisms used to blanket both genitalia and the sexual act itself.

Not that Brautigan's poems are simplistic, because they aren't. They're generally loaded little gems that are finely crafted with a sharp mind and a deft hand. Pretty astounding given he was (by all accounts) a total fuck-up in his personal life, a social misfit and an eventual suicide.

My wife read more poems aloud as we drifted toward LA. It was fun. After that, the book got stashed away somewhere (likely packed and disappeared along with my wife) and I forgot all about him. Years later the ghost of Richard Brautigan re-entered my life as required reading in a poetry class I was taking at SFU.

The name brought back some memories.

Have You Ever Been There?

after Richard Brautigan

"I lie here in a strange girl's apartment"

Something oddly familiar about this scene
has me adjust my crotch, sniff my fingers,
count the bills in my wallet, piece together
the lyrics from an old Beatles' tune:
    Isn't it good? Norwegian wood
listen for the splash of running water in the next room.
All of which, nonetheless, places the girl strictly
outside my personal frame of reference; outside, even,
the old familiar time/space continuum adjunct
ESSE EST PERCIPI
Attica, maybe, that beat path where the rich are
broad in guns & neck deep in bogus philosophy
aimed to level Flower Power
    & bust down doors of misconception.
Maybe San Fran. Big Sur. Tokyo. Babylon.
Or the abortion that was San Diego to Tijuana.
Or smoking the joint at the corner of Haight & Love.
Or taking a pull from a long neck somewhere in Montana.
Or simply baiting a line to trout fish in America.
In any case, things slowly curve out of sight
until they are gone: the girl, the tumbled sheets,
the Beatles, the apartment, even the cat that I had been
so sure was purring at my feet.
The entire works fold neatly into a Berkeleyan suitcase &
vanish
neat as anything.

Look! Birds fall from the trees &
the long strands of black hair I had picked from the pillowcase
loop branches & braid themselves a noose that promises
dreams
    of sweet cherry blossoms
        shot across a moonlit grave.

It Was Your Idea To Go To Bed With Her

after Richard Brautigan

"she wants candles married to her womb"

Given the subject
what was meant to be haiku
instead is Epic

Or …

Also trout beaded
around her wrists & ankles
to slip the grave moon

Or …

The match proves damp &
former whiskey sparks now blow
cold between the lips

Or …

CHARLES BUKOWSKI

Another *dirty old man* who reveals gold beneath the covers to anyone curious enough to claw the rough surface. Sure, Buk wrote a lot of crappy poems (who hasn't?) and he's frowned upon by the PCs – the 'culturally sensitive' we say today – still, he wrote a lot of great poems in the face of a public that shied away from his unapologetic bravado and his fearlessness in challenging the status quo and in continuing to write and submit his work even through the rejection.

Forgot, usually, is the fact that the man was well-read, well-educated *and he was not afraid to admit it*, both in his life and in his poems. This is a side I wanted to explore and present: the hard-drinking, cigarette smoking, gambling, womanizing poet jostling elbows with Freud, Mozart and Schopenhauer.

Strange bed fellows indeed.

warm exes

after Charles Bukowski

"how many dead beasts float and walk from Wales to
Los Angeles?"

there are those horses, those ones that boast a lineage,
that post as favourites, but finish dead last
no one questions
that stagger & drop at the wire in photo-ops of
delirious tremors
& shit ampoules of PCP out the ass of their dying
while we murdered tear up our ticket stubs
no one is surprised
we check our programs, ask about the wife, the kids,
ogle the tarted-up bleached blonde
with the duck lips & silicone tits
pressed tight to a player wearing a wedding ring
& two fingers jammed up her quim
lucky bastard
we scratch our bellies
& light our cigarettes for the next big fix
even as the twitching carcasses are dragged
to the local glue factory
no one is bothered
later, these brutes return to haunt
the glass of our beer mugs
they peer at us through eyes of warm exes
their noses daubed with angel dust
their horsey ears pricked with foam
their long faces bright with visions of
Eliot with his trousers rolled

Schopenhauer with his sufficient reason to exist
(beyond evil & loneliness, one guesses)
& what does it matter in the final dissolution?
snow fills the TV screens of America
& those horses, those ones with neither
a penny to spare nor a pot to piss in
kick up their ragged heels & shuffle off to Buffalo
we order more beer
no one gives a good flying fuck
cold in the knowledge:
            we recognize those faces
            we know those glue factories
            we are those horses

foolheart

after Charles Bukowski

> "each one
> gets a taste of honey
> then the knife"

day to day
no better or worse than any other, I suppose,
tarted up in the manner, as: still life with lions
sore afeared of fame
apparent indifferent to fortune's sugar tit
aroused necessarily by any fleshy redhead
clapped in *clickety-clack* high heels, hiked skirt,
tight sweater
flashing slim ankles, creamy haunches, watermelon
breasts, scarlet gash of hair lip
that bleeds
        "Nostradamus Nostradamus …"
between paper white thighs.

bow wow, bow wow wow

at night, the atmosphere grows haunted
& a jaundiced eye slits the shades.
inside, Mozart strains over staticky radio broadcast
Rimbaud spreads his sickness across the smoky table
the bath runs.
outside, bats dive-bomb the insect air
fabulous cats with electric tails & pinball eyes
yowl the litmus moon
dogs piss their shifty territory

grass & trees, fur & teeth
lamplight & fog.
elsewhere, Herr Freud sets a cheroot upon
his cancerous lip & blazes visions
of complex
Oedipus
a worn copy of Readers' Digest folded up his ass
a tattoo heart with "Mom" needled on his chest.

across the park, half the neighbourhood is drunk
the other half dead
the rest more or less engaged in the inaction.
they rattle sabres, gnash teats
dry hump the back seats of SUVs
high on the sniff of black leatherette panties
& baby blue exhaust.

who is willing to die for a six pack of Schlitz
a deck of Chesterfields, a brown paper bag of
California plonk
comes up short, in the end, & …
can a man actually sink through the skin
of his own ballooned belly?
drown among his own sacked entrails?
can his boiled potato balls never explode
like a pair of dangered hand grenades
to frighten away the mob?
can his spent liver never grow claws to tear apart
the fabled black bird
perched mocking the tip of his prick?
or is he, finally, alone naked in a room,
given to saw himself to death joint by joint
with a rat tail comb?
no one to hurl the radio out the window.

no one to slap closed the book.
no one to shut off the bath.
no nympho redhead to love him to sleep.
no one to explain to the worms & roaches:
this is not your fault. the universe goes on
forever, then it stops.
there are more killers than ever
& I write poems for them.

WILLIAM S. BURROUGHS

I came to appreciate Burroughs by slow degrees and probably more so as the character and/or persona who most represented the epitome of literary outlaw rather than as a writer *per se*: a bisexual genre-bending cat-loving gun-toting anti-establishment anti-censorship criminal element junkie whose family acquired its fortune by inventing the adding machine while he – along with Brion Gysin – invented the Dreamachine in order to experience altered realities. He also explored a cut-up technique in his writing similar to collage, a technique which I often employ in my own poems, though in a variation.

And, of course, there's that voice!

Disclaimer

after William S. Burroughs

"How I hate those who are dedicated to producing conformity."

First & final warning! If you have
epilepsy or any predisposition &/or otherwise
predilection toward seizures, blackouts, dizzy spells
&/or strokes &/or heart attacks &/or fallen arches
dandruff, genital warts, open lesions, weeping sores
or have trained your asshole to talk
or are of dubious character or have a criminal record
or claim to have been abducted by aliens
or plead a victim of circumstance, of fashion, of a frivolous
je ne sais quoi
or a casualty of an unforeseen decline in the stock market
or hostile takeover or downsized or made obsolete or deemed
necessary but not sufficient or declared legally insane
or on a mission from God
or on the dole, on the take, on the ropes, on the rag, on the nod
or are prone to either murder &/or suicide
or have intent toward malicious behaviour
or considered armed & dangerous
or keep a private journal &/or sketches with the prime purpose
of either:
                        public   display,   publication   &/or
                distribution
or have a monkey on your back, a horse in your arm
a rock up your nose, a gold bug up your sphincter
or are a mover, shaker, sweet little heartbreaker
or are generally melancholic or alcoholic

or a user
or have dreams of grandeur &/or aspirations toward immortality
or else feelings of depression &/or insecurity
or whack off to the strains of a star spangled banner
or whine that the drinks are watered
or masquerade as a paper tiger, a cardboard hero, a lipstick lesbian
or an identity crisis, such as: 'the artist formerly known as Prince'
or Madonna complex that drives a young lady *gaga*
or somehow believes the world owes you something
or complains that the spirit is willing but the flesh is weak
or if you are a total & absolute degenerate
or a complete asshole of the first order
or insist that: "Language is a virus from outer space"
yadda-yadda
or lisp, or drawl, or twang or else mutter incomprehensibly
or hum *The William Tell Overture* during coitus
or tend to belittle, bully or bullshit
do not (I repeat) do not engage, enter, &/or pass GO
do not (I repeat) do not collect either the 200 bucks
the all expense paid trip to Interzone, the free set of Ginsu knives
or the rough rogue trader equivalent

ignore the tall lank man behind the curtain!

there will be gunfire, there will be strobe lights, the smoke machine is in perfect working order, the adding machine is greased, the soft machine is functional, the Dream Machine is operational, cigarettes will be inhaled, there will be profanity rampant drug & alcohol use, full-frontal nudity, hyperbole, scenes of an explicitly sexual nature, random acts of violence, flagrant displays of self-immolation &/or spontaneous human combustion ritual Seppuku, near-death experience, the Indian rope trick, tubthumping, projectile vomit, the Heimlich maneuver

there will be blood

the views & ideas expressed are strictly those of the author & do not reflect the official party policy

the management is not responsible

the management is never responsible

remember these are paid trained professionals working under ideal conditions, do not try this at home

small children must be accompanied by an adult, all pets must be leashed, turn off any electronic devices, no photographs allowed

no one admitted once the doors are shut

no one permitted to leave once the lights fade to black

there will be no intermission

absolutely no refunds

ITALO CALVINO

A friend said I should read some Richard Ford. He thought our work had a lot in common. He said the two of us were both interested in writing about couples' relationships, especially in terms of sexuality. I picked up a copy of short stories and plunged in.

In the end I decided that I'd already written these same stories (OK, similar stories), only mine were shorter and better.

Not so with Italo Calvino. What do they say? That imitation is the sincerest form of flattery? After reading *Difficult Loves* I didn't want to imitate the man or his work, I wouldn't know how. Instead, I basically stole (yes, stole) one of his story ideas wholesale and set out to re-write it in my own fashion and make it mine.

Now, that's sincere flattery. And part of part of what's happening in "Broken Telephone."

Broken Telephone

after Italo Calvino

"In a network of lines that intersect"

or else they don't, or else they do, though imperfectly, or else
they might, if only, or else you'd wish them to, except, or
else a virus, or else "In a net worth of lies that interject," or
else (perhaps) interference by superior beings from another
planet, or else spiders high on LSD, or else radioactive waves
through phone cables that cause cancer of the brain, or else
"An ant works a lie that injures sex," or else invisible cities
within invisible provinces within invisible countries & so on,
or else difficult loves, or else "Anna irks allies at the inter-
text," or else a ghost writer in the machine, or else a famous
cosmic-comics dog that sits at a typewriter tapping out: *It was
a dark and stormy night* over & over, or else "Aunt warps lies
under threat," or else a man receiving scattered radio signals
via mercury fillings in his teeth, or else a telescope that bends
images, depending, or else a woman in a deck chair flipping
pages of a book wherein nothing's written, or else "Antwerp
dies a sudden death," or else …

RAYMOND CARVER

Have you ever had anyone say to you: you know, your writing reminds me of so-and-so's. Meanwhile, you have no idea who this so-and-so is and have never experienced their work on any level whatsoever … so far as you know.

'So far as you know' – an important concept to consider, since: no man is an island and no man is a windowless monad and Athena rarely (if ever) springs fully formed from the head of Zeus with a shout. Instead, there are predecessors (dead or alive/dead and alive) swirling in the ether that influence us whether we are aware of it or not. Sunspots were "discovered" in 1611 simultaneously in Italy, Germany, Holland and England. The invention of typewriting machines occurred simultaneously in America and England.

So it was with Ray, and, after I read him, I admit: yes, similarities. Differences as well. With his prose. With his poetry, two very different animals altogether. Hardly close and bearing little or no resemblance. Which is why I chose to write poems here rather than prose poems – no one is going to mistake me for him in this instance.

I think.

Head Above Water (Barely)

after Raymond Carver

"So much water so close to home"

What greater confluence
that creates
not so much the undertow
as the sheer dead weight
life being (they say) too
long for poetry, too short
for prose, suffers it:
the mixed blessing of children
(necessarily)
the piss-ass dog as well
that chews the crotches
out of the family clothes &
refuses to remain lost forever
the model wife unafraid to
bare a little tit now-&-again
or hike a skirt for sake of a
storied argument, the long
distant girlfriend whose creamy
thighs pine clamorous as the
Yellowstone
swelled (as ever)
to fuck the socks off
O Paradise, O Eureka
O hungered bite of the big apple
that proves less than other worldly
the Karmic backwash of stiffing
hired help at the Howard Johnson's

the bankrupt mortgage
the job that promises three squares
a day but starves the soul
the beat Nash Rambler
with its rear wheels stuck spinning
deeper into the river's bed
the tipped kayak, the string of
empty booze cans & bottles
the butt ends of cigarettes
the general all 'round poor white
attitude amid the swirl
the entire kit & kaboodle an anchor
tangled in fishing line, strung out
& knotted around kicked ankles
that bleed from the yank
mudsharks nosing his balls
rapids circling his neck
still alive (just) still breathing (barely)
the one who often mistook
diamonds for hearts & would
sudden drop tools, grab a bottle
drive 1200 drunken miles
Cupertino to Missoula
for a shot of real or imagined
strange piece of tail
no longer the Romantic notion
river rising, body sinking even as
the shadowy shape of some
prehistoric raptor long roosted
in the lungs is roused by the muddy
roil of tobacco smoke & gin
(go figure)
the aw shucks philosophic of it
mumbling: "Hey, gal!"

to the slipt ground that renders
situationlessness
a mean fact
madly paddling the churn above
while below, the eternal drag
nets little else save the invisible
                    human all too human
stings & terrors of egregious
misfortune

Running Dogs

"Music. Music! Everyone grew more famous"

Aroused by noise pitched outside the ken of mere mortals
They
Discover themselves sudden
      off the chain. Prick ears, bare teeth & put on the
Howl
Roam Palo Alto to San Fran. Let down hair (what remains)
Drop out. Tune in. Turn on
Their little things grow monstrous huge
In their wake a trailed spoor of oysters & beer
    prints the sandy North Beach toward City Lights. Tide high
Surf barks at heel. It utter bays. They prowl the
Hot spots with a thirst
Whiskey A Go-Go & the beautiful people. Women
In cages, men behind bars as if the most natural
Development
They pop cherries into Manhattans & chuff
Doors of perception crack to the naked scratch & sniff
Each dog a runaway. Each dog jail bait. Each dog a booze
hound
Set to paw the waitress, dry hump the hostess, piss
    in the first convenient fireplace. They raze flowerbeds
& perform their small function among the tulips
They quire on all fours & chorus a racket
Ah-rooo!
They lift a leg, mark territory, learn to lick their own balls,
make
With the perfect wolf whistle:

> "Hey, Blondie!"

Ghoulish apparition girdled alongside such other glamoured
Pusses in a crowd
Woof! Woof!

     (Terrored creatures twitch yellow eyed from upper tree
branches
     The hired help have it figured. They hide)

Eaches smell eaches asshole & get high on the odour
Where once upon a time their rhyme meant car fare (maybe)
Now a brief yelp demands big bones. Esquire, Playboy, GQ
They lay their haunches in pure gravy & lap it up
They tongue their whiskers
Life is sweet

& when the tooth grows long?
& when the tide ebbs?
& when the cherry bombs?
& when the music's over?
& when the last dog is hung?
What?

Fade away. Radiate
Fade away. Radiate

MONTGOMERY CLIFT

Monty's appeal to me was that he invariably played outsiders or victim-heroes and that his life mirrored tragic as his on-screen portrayals. For all his handsome leading lady's man hype, he was sickly, accident-prone and consequently hooked on alcohol and various pain killers. He was also rumoured to be gay at a time when this was anathema to Hollywood.

I guess my favourite scene comes from the movie *The Misfits* where he talks to his mom on a pay phone and you witness all the fear and insecurity emanate from Monty's gorgeous cowboy frame.

Marilyn Monroe was quoted to say: "He was the only one I knew who was in even worse shape than I was."

Cliffed

after Montgomery Clift

What it is that manufractures misfits of us all, *sans* make-up,
across the slippering plain (desert or some such strict romantic
notion alive with snakes, cacti, bucking broncs, mavericks &
further glued together [silica: not yet transparent, simply
shifting shifty-eyed in a blaze of sun; that heat hard upon & a
lit cigarette dangled at the lip]), spent surely as that nickel on
a call to home & ma hunched over the table peeling potatoes,
carrots, onions, foretelling a veritable feast with the legs cut
out from under, the joint slow-cooked around a camp fire,
later spooked up good & tight on fairy tales & corn liquor, the
grey matter addled, appearing like hot shit in spiked heels,
peek-a-boo bra, lace panties, a smear of scarlet across the
lips; Montgomery acting out the penultimate candle blown
three sheets to the freaky wind, his silver-screen ass sashaying
through the shimmered glass & fading to black in the distance.

LEONARD COHEN

On the one hand, difficult *not* to want to try and write a poem that concerns Leonard Cohen considering his unmistakable role as icon in Canadian poetry as well as the world of pop music. Conversely, these are the very things that prove fearful: how avoid simple mimicry, how avoid the problem of comparisons, how avoid accusations of name dropping? Though this should be the case for any poet writing on another poet, yes? Should be. Except this is LEONARD COHEN.

Beyond this gentle paranoia, my main reason for tackling Leonard is that way back in the '60s, during a grade 11 English class, we were descended upon by a student teacher who was the TV perfect image of those hippy-dippy days: young, blonde, blue-eyed, gorgeous west coast type wearing one of those loose fitting, tie-dyed dresses and beads and sandals and recently met with a broken leg accident on a ski trip, so sporting a hip-high plaster cast covered with gaudy coloured flowers, peace signs, paisleys and goofy well wishes and signatures.

All the boys in the class were in love (perhaps lust). All the girls were intrigued.

It was this young student teacher who dropped a vinyl album on a portable player and explained to us the close relationship between song and poetry and how this was epitomized in the works of Mr. Leonard Cohen.

And how could I not identify her with Suzanne and how could I not place my hand upon the thigh of poetry and not feel the thrill?

Suzanne Holds The Mirror

after Leonard Cohen

"because she's touched her perfect body
with her mind"

the difference between pop & poetry
makes for a thoroughly modern
milieu, the mirror held up to the
self image & no room for any other
narcissistic bent on resurrection
to crack the circle
O, how lend her a coin, Lazarus,
who has filled her pockets
with pennies
razed from the eyes of the dead
the whole town impresses
& the joint fairly bogarts with the buzz
as "we'll always have Paris"
takes on fresh meaning
bright new spirits
(not unlike Suzanne who, times passed, normal
would have faded to a haunt
    face caved, tits fallen, frame packed
        with a surplus forty ungodly pounds)
resurface fit as any saint whistled along
the boulevard *Haute Couture*
buffed, tanned, botoxed,
nipped & tucked
toting bite-sized mutts
designer cell phones
barely clad in:

rags & feathers lifted
   from Dolce & Gabbana counters
they are the model of perfection
apart any black weeded troubadour with desires
to eat each other out, whether on a bed of tea & oranges
or some other coarse Romantic rot
listen: singer breaks like the wind
crucifixion in hand, his throat a plague of frogs
his club foot dangled in the hell spent river
look: his brass eye opens to the world
& it is no blank reflection that procures
sailors to dance
   & song birds to sing in his anus.

The Singer Must Die

after Leonard Cohen

"No disease or age makes the flesh unwind"

What night nurse can accurate cure a sow of clouds, eh?
Tongues weep, sure & gravel-voiced singer must die,
this is only natural, as howls leaned hard upon the ground
unravel silky pearls before its whine & a koan
of pressed rainbows fuck a dropped purse.

Ground howls at this *hallelujah*: clouds dropped,
the night nurse learned to go on barefoot across
the gravel; lips burnt; rainbows pressed into the
stone tongue's weep.

Who by fire fail to account (ever) either monetary or
otherwise unsavvy gravel, lanyard dropped, coin ground
to howls, wicked nurse pressed in stone, famous blue
raincoat rivered into night even as noosed tongues weep
rainbows amid the inglorious clouds.

Dropped on this gravel-ground stone, night howls among
clouds pressed to nurse a rainbow's weep, Leander, say,
coined stiff as stone among hero's beautiful losers.

No home with a hard-on tongues clouds instead of gash,
price of a member dropped in value alongside pressed
rainbows & laundered coins. Ground howls empty in the
night even as sisters of mercy clamp, twist thumb screws,
nurse gravel through the catheter.

Neither borrower nor lender coincided at this cashed cow.
Whether dropped ground or stone 'pressed clouds, each
nurse tongues gravel even as night howls & rainbows weep.

STANLEY COOPERMAN

I didn't know Stanley nor did I ever take a class with him at SFU. By the time I'd started there, he was already a suicide and all that remained was the myth – the stories behind the man – and a couple of books of poetry.

Apparently, he was a bit of a guru/Svengali to his students and was an especially seductive figure to the young women in his class. He reportedly managed to talk at least one of these women into dressing in a sheer slip, step out of a third floor window and walk along the edge of the building "as if sleepwalking."

He was probably one of the few (if not only) Jewish Surrealist poets on the west coast. He also wrote a number of poems that dealt with either food or eating.

A man of appetites.

Kitsilano Beach

after Stanley Cooperman

"Everything I do is a kind
of eating"

you would prefer to be a hot dog stand vendor
smoking cigarettes naked in a cloud of propane
frying onions in the pomegranate wind
licking mayonnaise from the chins
of pretty girls with
sauerkraut breath
apricot skin
breasts the firmness of hard-boiled eggs
their chocolate-y rosebud nipples discreetly
camouflaged by green & red parrots
that squawk
      Leonard Cohen
      Leonard Cohen
among the fig leaves

you would prefer to be a blood hound
let off the chain to sniff
the marmalade thighs & strawberry crotches
of legal secretaries clam-shelled in grey mini-skirts
their ankles sleek as oysters slipt across the boardwalk
the ones with hot apple sauce in their veins
who laugh behind the snap of juicy fruit gum
their clitoral tongues flapping red as grapes
in the dark orchards of their mouths
their almond-shaped assholes
itchy with garlic pork folded

into the eyes of barn owls

you would prefer to scour the mashed potato shore
hunched over bare knees & knuckles
cut to the quick by barnacled rocks
stuffing pockets with washed-up condoms
that stomach
    Japanese cherries
        Indian curry
            Italian ice cream
                Russian caviar
                    Yiddish gefilte fish
                        Norwegian herring
                        French cheese
                          German sausage
                      Spanish rice
                Chinese noodles
              Canadian back bacon
            American pie
        Irish potatoes
      Scottish salmon
    Welsh rarebit
along with the more traditional take-out
chicken entrails, tea bags, orange peels
pubic hair
olive pits the appearance of cancerous testicles
rusted hand guns
meant to make a *megillah* out of

instead, the blue speckled trout
you forked into your mouth
has spawned wooden bullets
in the buttery sea spray of your candied skull
they navigate the brainpan clacking with the precision

of pneumatic teeth
set to grind flesh & bone to a pulpy mass
ashes to ashes, dust to dust
see: your vampire skin flakes to pastry
under the yolk-yellow moon
&

       (who thought nothing better than
       to suck mock turtle soup through a straw
       or sink fangs into the neck of his own
       soiled underwear)
eats himself ape-shit at the edges

JULIO CORTAZAR

The novel *Hopscotch* is one of my all-time favourites and I re-read it every few years. It's Paris, of course, and Argentina and jazz and literature and philosophy and sex and a lost tragic soul traversing and commenting on these worlds. It's also written in such a manner as to be read either straight through front to back or else by hopping back&forth/in&out following directions listed at the end of chapters (which include deleted sections while also eliminating whole other sections.)

It's also a book about language and playing with language. In this prose poem (as well as other pieces in this collection) I use Julio Cortazar's name and create several fractured homonyms in order to mirror this playfulness.

The Little Corpse

after Julio Cortazar

"What good is a writer if he can't destroy literature?"

What it is that begins as a stone-cold raw potato question *by &
by* transcribes a more fluid dictation, say: music, tra-la-la. Jazz,
mainly: Ma Rainey, Big Bill, Bessie, Satchmo, Oscar, though, the
classics: Brahms, Dèlibes, Saint-Saëns. Jazz, mainly, though,
Kant, Cunningham, Brecht, Bergman. Jazz, mainly, though, the
usual bullshit *conversation* (touch upon politics; touch upon
religion; touch upon travel, lineage, suicide; glom onto sex;
especially sex; remain with sex). Jazz, mainly, though, Freud &
his shadowy bridges. Jazz, mainly, though, the Surrealist bent for
placement of disparate objects side by each or the construction
of boxed forms suspended by the slightest threads, as:

the bride stripped bare by her bachelors

or to look at the world through the eye of your asshole causes
quite a flap in the sails of the base subscribership, the prone
figure stretched immobile across the sheets, one foot toed
toward heaven, the other dangled tentative above the Seine,
the champ marshalled outside the academy left to marvel
endgame a lifetime, never mind hands cupped in the shapes
of breasts or bodies convulsed with a taste for monkey shines
or tongues twisted in an effort to disarticulate *con* from *coq* or
the ancient skill of carving flesh from bone that involves strict
usage of a set of tiny knives nested in the manner of Russian
matryoshka dolls whose sole purpose is to decompose an
exquisite corpse (some *thing* being rotten in the state, meant,
meaning …?) or Champion Jack Dupree plunked smack in the

green candled glow wailing: *So long, whiskey, so long ver-mouth,* prepped, as ever, to give it up & abandon wreckage, walk the so-called sober straight & narrow *as if* or his face ready to fly off its hinges at the retelling presents a riddle wrapt in an enigma rolled inside a paradox that concedes the entire dark continent gone Gliglish. How manage to resolve transfer of meaning with so much unsaid one thing before &/or after the other? Hey! say: Sanskrit, say: Rosetta, say: desire, say: love confuses amid the toss of Oriental carpets, Czech vodka & French fried potatoes.

No doubt aware that to translate is to betray cannot prevent the kiss spent naked upon the lips or that little death that so literally comes close at heel (euphemistic *le petit mal*) barely doing justice to the act. Beware the Jabberwock, my son, for, the only imperative categorical to speak of, remains: gloves dropped, wrists strapped, mouths gagged, blindfolds secured, bodies bared, skin lubed, coffee put to boil, ritual cigarettes lit while (in the heat of it) fucks up. Such was/is the moral sickness blown out of all proportion.

Who laid low to court a star was not the jewel, O, of the Côte d'Azur, instead, an itinerant stranger hopscotched Buenos Aires to Paree & back. Slaved to Pascal's unknowing how to begin until one ends is discomfited by the least line of inquiry; begs a strange blend of calculating cats, bagged nails, linked sausages, yards of folded gabardine, sepia faded photographs, pebbles dropped from windows into the square & kicked around the block; the reduction of volumes to their most plaintive, primal bawl:

Where is La Maga?

DON DELILLO

I was asked to act in DeLillo's play, *The Day Room*, around the same time that his novel *Underworld* came out. I liked the play and figured I'd give the book a read since I was unfamiliar with his work. One glance at the sheer bulk of it and I thought, maybe I'll begin with something a bit more portable. I picked up a copy of *White Noise* which I thoroughly enjoyed, then went on to read the rest of DeLillo, including the massive aforementioned *Underworld*.

I think what I enjoyed most in *White Noise* was DeLillo's description of the physical effort and contortions it took for the lead character to attempt to learn to speak German.

I also performed this piece as part of a dance/art/spoken word project in Basel, Switzerland in the summer of 2009.

Say It

after Don DeLillo

"We began to marvel at our own ability to manufacture awe"

guttural almost ragged almost raw almost savage almost
violent almost foreign almost an excess almost an exercise –
the tip of the tongue the teeth the lips – almost an exorcise
an exhortation an exhalation almost a language calcified turgid
rubbery gelatinous stringy the tongue the tongue a clawed
coarse fanged furred slouched rough beast drowned almost
almost awash in spit spittle sputum mucus gobsmacked the
agglutinate hack of blood-streaked phlegm the non-stop glottal
the vainglorious attempt to get the lips pursed the mouth
around the teeth sunk into amid the thrash the kick the gnarl
the tumble the word-spurt the word-sperm the word-spunk
entered & entering between the jambs uncomfortable uneasy
sure go on go on yeah go ahead do it do the business do the
chore do the works do the deed do the do do the nasty do
the naughty do the trick do the hanky-panky do what don't
come natural go on go on say it say it Bill say *no ideas but in
things* say Sablatnig-Beuchelt why not? say Sachsenring say
Slaby-Beringer say Scheibler say Solidor say Sperber say Staiger
say Staunau say Steudel say Stoewer say Stolle say Szawe say
*there are more things in heaven & earth than are dreamt of in your
philosophy Horatio* say Scheler say Schiller say von Schlegel say
Schleiermacher say Schlick say Schopenhauer say Schottlaender
say Schmidt say Schulze say Steiner say Stirner say Stumpf say
Shtupp go on go on try cough it up spit it out exhaust it the
contrails of language hung up in the mist in the fog in the
suspended particulate in the dangling participle in the dangling

conversation exhausting exhaustive exhausted the great white noise that emanates never one word where a dozen will suffice hey what's the matter? what's the problem? what boots? what's the buzz? don't you understand? don't you get it? can't you dig it? where's your sense of humour in all this? are you thick? häsch du es Brett vor ein Chopf? are you Germanophobic? do you have a two-by-four nailed to your forehead? don't dial hello if you don't want to linger don't want to languor don't want to lingua franca cha-cha-cha pay no attention to the little man behind the curtain Adolf Hitler say stood waving stiff-backed from the jump seat of a gun barrel grey Mercedes Benz his palms unfurled like lamps spotlighting lips that flap madly in the breeze beneath the infamous black mustachio say look! say listen! see it see the spray wash over the awed crowd say it say häsch du es Brett vor ein Chopf? say it go on say it say shower say *sig heil* say shot to hell say holy *scheisse*

say the false bottom drops out the character utter disappears except as image except as archetype except as trace matter except as discourse except as curiosity except as thing except as history taken for a joy ride tugged along on the caped back of Captain Marvel go ahead go on say it say it say it say it say it say it say it say it say it say it say it ...

T. S. ELIOT

Probably one of the most (perhaps *the* most) influential poems on me, and the poem which further stirred my interest in poetry and writing poetry myself, has to be *The Love Song of J. Alfred Prufrock*. The poem struck me as a sort of portmanteau squashed full of imagistic delicacies lifted from history, art and literature.

Along with the allusions and metaphors and comparisons to real and fictional characters, I also love the outright sampling of lines from the so-called "great" works: the Bible, Dante, Shakespeare, Marvell and so on. Eliot manages to beg, borrow and steal from numerous other texts and combine them in such a manner as to make the poem his own.

I attempt to do somewhat the same.

They Called Me The Hyacinth Girl

after T.S. Eliot

"Who walked between the violet and the violet"

What an Opera! What an Opera
       buffa who ate toast & tea at
the cocktail party
who walked between the violins & the violence
who walked between the knack & the knackered
who walked between the art & the artifice
moving through the flagrant white & blue-petalled
      the violet, the blood red
his mouth choked with dried tubers
talking base matter. Butt-ends;
a call for fiddlers & skin flutes in the pit

What an Opera! What an Opera
      addict screaming bloody blue murder
in the cathedral
who longed to lay down the lyre in exchange for
the favours of a youth laid naked, sleeked with oil
alive in a field of muscari, skin soft as baby's breath
lips hung violet as grapes in the afternoon sun

'Tis a hell of a lot to expect of one neither Prince Hamlet
nor attendant lord, more, the fop arrayed in ladies finery
positioned at the merchandise table hawking flowers:
      pansies for you, that's thoughts, & hyacinths
      & daisy chains for me, & rosemary for … for …

What an Opèra! What an Opèra
            bouffe where gods fall to mortals upon this stagy
waste land
old possum, breasts saggy, violets withered, member
cinched to a *V* between his legs
grown bored, turned his hand to sport & wasn't bad.
Hurled the discus with strength enough to cut a cloud in two.
Not without its melodrama, music crescendos & tale purples
as woodwinds (full of jealous rage) blow a youth to ecstasy
& spin an aged man grave, death come as a whimper not a bang
head bent in rapturous supplication moving between
            the white & blue-petalled, the violet, the blood red

Pinned

after T.S. Eliot

"Like a patient etherised upon a table"

Not suddenly. Not that.
Death being a paper cut in the brain
Lingers exacts its pounded flesh
by slow degree: life, half-life & so on
to the quick
aware each seven brutal years
the body fabricates new skin
until it no longer suits. At this post-mortem
begins the visions
                        air turns blue
the slot packs in measured coffee spoons
mad faces fly in sundry mad direction
chess men scuttle claws across the ragged board
nurses frail as dust bunnies come & go, go & come
cradling withered breasts in weathered hands
their violet mouths violent with recollections
(not "O O O O that Shakespeherian Rag")
no, of thoroughly modern
                        hurried sucks & second hand fucks
good-night ladies, sweet ladies
meanwhile, it's moist Ophelia holds the mirror
at such a dark   either my self-portrait
or some other spit image. Look! I dreamt
I took it to the beach; fed it tea & oranges
laid it out nice & corpse-like 'neath the sun.
What else had I done wrong & who died on account?
Evening saw blankets kicked feverish from the bed

saw a pink glow pulse the pale white sheets
saw the beat of wings
        as the chest rattled & the lungs collapsed
saw the room quiver a storm of ash-dry skin
& then, what wonders
(where the ghost of a well-mowed
        skull might give cause to make one cry)
a slippering design aroused upon the breeze
took shape of an old man spiked with cigarette eyes
smoky teeth, fog-yellow beard, a god (perhaps) returned
in the re-turning, mesh net in one hand, bent pin in the other
he fingered his parched lips, leaned across the guts, sucked
the breath dry, tittered:
        Sh! Tom sees moths.

MARIANNE FAITHFULL

I was at a party in a Commercial Drive apartment, Vancouver, circa 1980, say, and someone put on a smuggled version – banned in Canada! – of *Why'd Ya Do It?* and suddenly all the women in the room started jumping around like mad and having a helluva good time singing along. They had all the lyrics memorized and acknowledged this song as a *wimz-lib* anthem and direct assault against the low-life bastard males of the world.

Who the hell is this, I asked? Marianne Faithfull? Yikes! The only tune I knew from her was *As Tears Go By* when she was still dating Mick Jagger. Her voice had grown harsher, growlier, more worldly, more world weary, apparently due in great part to a steady diet of drugs, alcohol, tobacco and heart break.

This song (this album) was definitely a very large step in a very different direction.

I saw her give a live performance years later at The Phoenix Club in Toronto – just her and a guitar player – fantastic!

A Child's Adventure

after Marianne Faithfull

"Alcohol can take you there"

Or a kidnapped buss
            that entrances a *not-so-magic* mystery tour
Hooks our fair sister morphing 'tween
Heavy traffic (yes?)
Convent to bordello without appeal
Neither a hamlet's broke English nor the mantled gaslight
Items coined to nick her jag merely drive her to the fateful
Edge
I mean, what rude spectacle clapped in daisy chains
Cinches a sweet girl's rosebud in squeaky leather
Spreads her thighs around a hog's head
& spikes a needle through her vein
                        as price of commission
Too bad, so sad
All those blue millionaires sat in the blue dark
Strapped to the arms of blue chairs
Pansies a'bloom in their broad blue lapels
Their breath raspy with the slow blue burn of cigar smoke &
whiskey
Their lit cigarette eyes prepped as ever
                            to drill blue holes in tendered flesh
Strange weather indeed that streams a brain with storm clouds
Forces lips to go down on this false erection
Fame
            (a fair thought to lie 'twixt maid's legs)
What becomes the music in this wat'ry flow
Emerges flip side some wholly altered

Who is Ophelia & knows what it is to be mad
Wears her rue with a difference
Coughs up the bloodied goods

> *O, before you tumbled me*
> *You promised me to wed*

Sings hey non nony, nony, hey nony
Brings an end to all violet visions
An end to all grave
Flowers

JUDITH FITZGERALD

The first book I picked up and read by Judith Fitzgerald (quite by accident, as I had no idea who she was) was *Lacerating Heartwood*. Here were poems that were dark, sexy, funny, dangerous, personal (shall I say confessional? yet with an eye (an ear) cocked toward a vaster picture), composed with rare intelligence and a real feel for language, wordplay, rhythm, precision and sense of 'literariness'. Toss in the fact that she was a fan of Leonard Cohen, T.S. Eliot, Country & Western music, bowling and I was hooked. I went searching for more books. No easy task given that Judith is a Canadian poet living in Canada, meaning: bookstore shelves – tiny places in back corners somewhere even the staff have difficulty locating and generally filled with dusty copies of British (perhaps American) poets, the Classics – wasn't much help.

I persisted and managed to accumulate a fair-sized collection, all the while wondering – why isn't this poet and her work more well-known and well-respected? OK, *yeah-yeah*, beside the fact that very few poets achieve anything of this sort in our country. Still. She had, after all, hung and wrote with many of our more (today) recognizable poets, so, what gives?

Apparently, she managed to piss a lot of people off over her career and for various reasons, so maybe that's it, why she's been overlooked. In an artistic climate that demands polite personable company, she made herself un-fit. Maybe. Beyond, though, is the work itself, which I try to celebrate whenever possible.

Cheers, Judith.

Once In A Blue Moon

after Judith Fitzgerald

"What I need to write I write around"

What makes suggestive more than all the tease in China
assumes positions reversed : stood alone
      no dream in her heart, no love of her own
old maverick moon hung like an oyster in the blue
skirt hiked, panties torn, trousers dropped
taken up the ass with a stiletto heel
pale reflection : self &/or other : heartfelt
dreamer, beautiful loser, teenage wasteland
little or no desire to be a pair of ragged claws
scuttling this or any deeper salty bed
mind the gap
    where blues train comes up short (again)
& every cowboy mouth blows homoerotic
in the re-mix, back broke by that distant range
Montes Cordillera
Spanish tongue slipped, & – not that there's anything
wrong with that, just …
you still taste the boots, still get a kick, still two-step
that dance to the end of love. Bitter? Better.
Took a lickin', went on tickin'
So long, sport! Adios, Kemo Sabe. Hasta luego, baby.
Don't care if it rains or freezes, long as I've got my
plastic Jesus
we just want the facts ma'am
        no CSI Miami gathering lurid skin particles
fingernails, semen, pubic hair
no yellow fog rubbed against the glass

simple testimony; DNA of word made stone; a life
measured in coffee spoons & cigarette butts
where what begins in the sack sniffing various privates
ends (finally) as a friendly foursome on the golf course.
Sure. Don't we all. Too late to redress; to redefine :
            "all you ever do is bring me down"
Blue Moon. You saw me. Sawed me.
Being, *O*, not what I meant, not what I meant at all.
Tears it.

SIV CEDERING FOX

I stumbled across a book of poems accompanied by black and white drawings (or a book of black and white drawings accompanied by poems) titled: *The Juggler,* and felt an immediate kinship with the author. I thought wouldn't I be nice to try and get in touch with her and at least let her know that I enjoyed her book. The only thing I knew about the poet was that she lived in New York State. This was before the time of Google, you understand, in the Stone Ages, when people still had private lives.

I sent a letter to the publisher asking if they would forward it to her. Some time later, a letter arrived from Siv – a delightful letter. It was our only correspondence, though memorable for it having happened at all.

I've sent letters more recently to others from whom I've received no response, whether due to the publisher's disinterest or the writer's, I don't know.

A quick Google informs me that Siv went on to write 20 books and had a novel turned into a screenplay directed by Sven Nykvist which won an Academy Award for best foreign film in 1991 – holy cow! Also found out she died in 2007 at the age of 69. Maybe too much information.

Siv's work often deals with dreams, sleep, darkness and I've tried to combine these themes with the cover drawing of *The Juggler*.

When The Night Is Still

after Siv Cedering Fox

"But the angel of death is somewhere,
watering my flowers"

Ever. Ever. Ever
between the light light & the dark dark
indeterminate dusk insinuates
        its juggled act of balls & breasts
performs its awed acrobatic
picture a stalked figure caught *just so*
not another tall cool glass of water
stood unaffected at the echoed edge
rather, a body wrapped ecstatic in pallid leotard
the back arched & (as if in the very throes)
the head tossed back, the hair let down, the milky neck
exposed to whatever night shade
the tempered chest swollen
    slight; slightly
            barely nippling the fabric
arms are bent stems creeping toward filigree fingers
which unfurl in the shape of wings
            a vase of narrow hips bone the sunk belly
            the flat ass
            the crotch images a narcissus bulb
            struggling to surface
within this upset frieze
who would desire to slip its tight skin
is burned at both ends
below, a tattoo of hands grips the calves & root the legs
above, what might be taken for a black glove clapped

across the hungered mouth
       is a shadow leaned liquid from the flowered curtain
pouring itself either
                    into or out of
the petalled lips

MERLE HAGGARD

All the stories they tell about Merle are true, except those that are not. Same with Johnny Cash, who never "shot a man in Reno just to watch him die" and, so what? That's what makes art *ART* and reality whatever the hell it is. Beyond this, both artists are definitely outsiders in terms of society and CW music (though embraced and slotted in the end, which is the real authentic American way, after all, yes?).

Given that I appreciated Merle's dark, dramatic, existential/ philosophic side, my idea was to try and position him further into the more literary canon (alongside man-in-black Johnny Cash), by inserting him (his life) alongside Camus' *The Stranger* and Shakespeare's *Hamlet* and *Macbeth* (which are also touchstones for me, anyway).

I don't know if it works. I hope.

The Outsider

after Merle Haggard

> "I turned twenty-one in prison
> doin' life without parole"

Strange. Stranger. Not Camus, though parallel
Arrested action. In any case, a bust with convention
Which ends
         a head on the block.
Nothing the French invented.
Workin' man blues, & so on. On the prowl.
Nose for news, & so on. Also on the prowl.
All so loosely translated, begins:
        In the beginning was the word
Defines:
   "… actual linguistic behaviour or performance of individuals
     in contrast to the linguistic system of a community …"
Outlaw existential
Ism
Momma barely dead & buried
Sparks a reefer, drinks a café au lait, goes for a swim
Fondles the butt'ry thighs of a moist young gal in the back row
   of a darkened movie theatre
Fails to unriddle
The comedy of a crucifix hung like a dagger in the flick'ry light
& what was it someone said? Reading a translation
Is like fucking a bride through a horse blanket?
Nay, too rude a remark for Pablo who rarely (if ever) kissed
Down between the stems on paper or any otherwise public
Prison.
Then?

Heaven knows momma tried, momma tried.
Now left to the blear and roar of ocean. Knows (as well)
The world is inarticulate, friend, & a recurrent car wreck.
Who learned to drink bourbon neat, tap ashes in the beer for
strength
Can only reconfigure
If a single bullet does the trick
What boots this desire to plug further, except,
No desire?
Funereal meats coldly furnish forth the execution.
Man in black sing:

>*Shot a man in Reno, just to watch him die*

Time being out of joint axes it.
Crucifix hung like a dagger in the flick'ry light.

DEBORAH HARRY

Beyond a great set of pipes and music that adjusted to the times under the influence of pop, rock, punk, jazz, Reggae … who could forget that photo of her clad in slight white dress and white shoes leaned against a rooftop wall?

Then there's the story of how the band got its name.

Poets' Problem

after Deborah Harry

"I think I'll do a line, then again"

Tell me about it. Beyond base need for more lead in the pencil situates the matter most definite *out-of-reach* in this artless time/space continuum. Here exists the rapture that separates & renders every longing unfulfilled. I mean, how frame this bonsai baby who refuses to disappear behind the make-up except as myth? Except as moth laid out upon the glossy spread then pinned down between the dusty sheets of the girl next door? Whether chaste or chased, who did bare a whorey "B" side against the usual virgin record crowd is framed a'glimmer with platinum hair, pearl necklace, vanilla armband, silver bracelet, bleached stiletto heels & a paper-thin white dress that downright nipples in the breeze; virtually begs to be ripped to shreds & scattered cherub-like from the rooftops. Pain in the ass, perhaps, fielding catcalls from brain-smoked cigarette-thin lone wolves perched on street corners of Union City Blues, hunkered behind wheels of wide-finned Chevvies, leaned demonic from cherry-bomb Buick windows, spanking door panels with grease-stained hands, bruising air with profane odours of stale beer, crusty back seat sex, gawd awful poetry & exhaust, yet –

What punch-drunk bravado that hollered a name & struck a chord: "Hey, Blondie!"

Blunt phrase of simple hard-on-wired male hormone nailed in the flesh of it & no way/no desire to avoid either the lyric wet dream spent peeked through the shower curtain or lesser evil that makes the scene with a magazine or else the: "I know but I don't know" *possibility* gone deaf, dumb & blind from the harried debris of five finger exercise. The problem being – caught up in the eye-candied rub & tug – almost (almost) ignores the heartfelt naked voice laced with cyanide, packed with powder, touched by the flap of snowy wings & armed with enough necessary evil to cause any atomic angel to take flight, soar:

> fade away & radiate
>   fade away & radiate
>   fade away & radiate ...

TED HUGHES

It's been about 30 years since I smacked into Ted Hughes' marvellous collection "Crow" and it continues to affect me. He somehow managed to take this archetypal/mythical character and re-dress it as his own. No mean feat. I say 'somehow' because I couldn't begin to say how this effect was accomplished overall. I know the image I had in my mind reading the poems was that of an all-powerful being, full of piss and vinegar, with a cigar stuck in its mouth and wearing a rumpled raincoat, much like Detective Columbo (or perhaps Charlie Chaplin's little tramp), though absentmindedly burping, farting, eating and fucking its way through the processes of life & death.

So taken was I by the collection that I wondered: how can anyone dare use the image of a crow ever again in a poem? In fact, I avoided it in my own work for the longest time. Used raven, used blackbird, used starling. Did not use crow. At some point I figured, time to get over this; you can't be afraid forever; other poets are using the goddamn image; it's only a word *fer chrissakes*!

OK, I began to introduce the word slowly back into my vocabulary and it wasn't so bad. Hardly frightening at all. Hardly. Though I did still look at it and wonder if it actually stood up to … you know … CROW, in capital letters.

Which lead to the creation of this poem. My attempt to re-claim the word and move on. We'll see how it fares 'out there' in the real world.

You Are Beautiful

after Ted Hughes

"Then everything went black"

If I say: don't imagine the word "crow"
gray matter fairly convulses with the dark intrusion; revels
in this smudgy form that hacks blood, coughs up entrails,
brandishes its prick in the fashion of
　　　　a ceremonial Japanese decapitator bent on distinctness,
its hairy balls hung sombre as lampshades beneath the
insurrection.

If I warn: don't, above all, imagine the word "crow"
it's already too late. The murky figure slips its inky cloak,
scorches the brainpan with a hot piss of cigarettes & whiskey.
Its gritted teeth erect a cliff that grinds the skull to *papier mâché*.
Busted loose, it swathes an uncivil path across the carpet &
　　　　(never certain whether to kill its father & fuck its mother
　　　or the reverse)
drags its blind carcass through the first unlit doorway.

If I plead: don't, under no circumstance, imagine the word "crow"
the damage is done. Nothing contains this shape
　　　　　　　　　　　　that isn't ripped asshole to teacup.
Brothers & sisters eat each other out with unnatural hunger.
Favoured aunts & uncles suicide.
Heads tumble from necks at the least flap of sharp, black
feathers.
Vulvas bleed complex Oedipus onto bed sheets.

Drawing room curtains shudder with the spraddle of ragged-
clawed
genitalia bawling:

> *momma … momma …*

Ah, my old darling etcetera
in whose dead shoes I take a walk out of the air
& am made grave
      you are beautiful.

JACQUIE JACOBS

Difficult to know how or where to start with this: my Muse, my mouse, I was *enamoured* with her lusty beauty and energetic personality – RED – before I discovered she was also a terrific artist (luckily), which only served to fuel the attraction.

I say 'luckily' because it's too often the case that you meet someone and there is that initial spark and they eventually say, oh, I'm an artist, I'm a writer, I'm a poet, I'm an actor (or whatever) *too* and they want you to look at/read/watch and comment favourably and the work is dreadful and immediately the spark sputters and quickly dies as there is no way to keep up the pretence of "Oh, yes, very nice, I like it, it's … interesting, it's …"

You're lost and nothing to do except pack your toothbrush and leave.

Not so with Jacquie who continues to amuse and amaze.

Sanguine Odalisque

after Jacquie Jacobs

"Breasts are funny things. When mine grew,
my feet disappeared"

What becomes a foreign body most.
What does, beyond the obvious idyll spread?
Titian hair
   coralline cheeks
      crimson lips
         raspberry nipples
           florid thighs
               her harried gash blooms moist magenta
         flushed legs
      cabernet ankles
   scarlet nails
Makes most becoming. Comes to it with a vengeance.
Parts abstract or no.
How exotic this madder matter that puts on the reveal
In broad strokes.
More Behmer than Ingres. More Klimt than Behmer.
More Jacobs than Klimt.
Ah, strange familiar! Who sings the electric bawdy
   to landscape
      poised for any severed transliteration.
Whether *Weltanschauung* or *réchauffé*
Nothing shies within this frame that bleeds a canvas
Red, red, red.

As what may greet the red model too
Insinuates the very heart, hung as she is & mounted

All most metonymic, meaning: odd & in love at worst,
   at best, is dropt square in the tits of it
      apprised for every vagrant eye to behold.
Background become foreground & vice versa.
As Paris. As Berlin (already burning) adds fuel to a fire
No simple splash of feet can douse.
As music, even, meant to calm the savage breast
Turns its back in a sulken rage.
Rages
As the stone grave robber meant to whistle
                      down, wanton, down
Blushes red outside the heat-fogged window.
As more time spent horizontal than vertical
   blows hot jazz through skin flute & hair comb
     & makes inflammatory.
Remarks upon the age of a scent.
Cinnamon, say. Say, cardamom. Say, curry.
Comes on. Comes on like gangbusters.
Images the mirrors a blaze of rusty visions.
Naked bodies bruised red & stoked by the titular
Romantic
Notion:
   dirty French postcards
     drawn toward yet another
       German Dance of Death
As amid the frantic gnash of teats & grind of privates
(which, normal, represent a proper gallery viewing)
Lids close. They utter shut.
& feet?
Feet *disparu* in a kick of covers hot as hell
All bright & knocked soft-shoed off to Buffalo.

FRANZ KAFKA

I took a creative writing course with J. Michael Yates a few centuries ago and he presented us with a list of recommended reading. The list went on for pages and pages and contained books and authors that I was generally unfamiliar with on any level whatsoever. Even the handful I recognized, I hadn't read more than a few (though in some cases, I'd seen the movie so at least had a slim notion of what was going on) and these few fell in the Science Fiction category: Bradbury and Asimov, say.

Suddenly I was introduced to people like Donald Barthelme, Robert Coover, Julio Cortazar, Franz Kafka ... to name a few.

I read up on Kafka and got the typical background story of dark, moody, existential, tragic, sickly, metaphorical and so on – pretty scary heady stuff for a guy who worked in a bowling alley.

Then I plunged into the man's actual writing and found that not only could I identify with these stories and these situations, I found them to be (more often than not) dryly amusing and was pleased to see that Kafka had a sense of humour and playfulness about him. He wasn't simply this big impenetrable black cloud rolling around the sky set to blast a poor naive reader senseless with a rain of brimstone and fire.

Or was it just me? I braved my way onward.

The Trial

after Franz Kafka

"Like a dog"

By his own hard reckoning, judged barely more substantial than a cough, really. Thin, pale as a sheet & scant vision of any Amerika bucket ride that might include either an inscrutable father figure or red wheelbarrow glazed in rainwater surrounded by white chickens. Rather, a few roses splashed onto a linen handkerchief that imaged a single bleak portrait of the artist as a little dickens who trumpeted the circus that was *The Nature Theatre of Oklahoma* for comic relief far beyond the grave limits of Prague. Far beyond a critique of pure reason, as well (macabre asylum where he & his ghoul dabbed make-up on their unmade faces so as to appear half-ways presentable to the mob). The works smacked of nonsense. Beyond (also) fear & trembling & the sickness unto death, only too well aware that when you are sore & kick a dog, the thing recurs to haunt. Even with his neck under heel of the laws, the loss, was not enough. Not nearly. Philosophy or whatever further human ailment – God, say, caught forever with its horn rammed in the burning bush – reduced to vitreous humour. Sound the alarm, Marla! The joint is jonesed & a man's home is no longer his castle. Whose own categorical imperative: to be shot down in flames, sentenced to ashes, reduced to a cancelled cheque, was instead convicted & condemned to the confines of a dusty shelf. What new hell was this? His coffined body (propped & supported between the stiff broad shoulders of O, James Joyce & O, Immanuel Kant), coughs.

Castle Keep

after Franz Kafka

"I like the Americans because they are healthy and
optimistic"

See! He rides his girl
never
proposes out
both sides of his mouth
the im/possibility
neither
red-blooded nor
American, seems
        (being there by chance)
instead
a sour & quirky
gardener
leap-frogged
toward the abyss
he sips his beer
bleeds words
onto crisp
white sheets

      his bed bugs
      bigger than
      their bed bugs

he appears
the original (as in)
un-holy ghostly

fatal "K"
&
> could we be more amazed
> by a man

if his heinie
retched
Nice cheese
or bowler hats flew
out his shirt collar
or sanatoriums sprung from
his ears
not home, home on the range
he is content
in the furthest recess
in the furthest drawer
in the furthest desk
in the furthest corner
in the furthest room
in the furthest castle
of the furthest kingdom
Amerika

JACK KEROUAC

On The Road is another book I came to late. I approached it cautiously and with a large grain of salt. After all, there was the matter of the myth to consider and how manoeuvre through that kind of grand hype?

Not so problematic, really, like putting on a comfortable pair of pants: one leg at a time. And it was a great ride. As was *Desolation Angels*. As was *The Subterraneans*.

And that voice! I was given a set of tapes as a Xmas present from my mom and listened as he riffed to the accompaniment of a couple of his hero jazz musicians – Al Cohn and Zoot Sims. Listened then read the liner notes as he got drunker and drunker trying to impress them and how, at the end, the musicians finished their gig, collected their money, packed their instruments and left him there on the floor in tears, unrecognized, alone. After all, who was this Jack Kerouac character anyway?

He wanted to talk, they were already thinking about their next gig.

Heart breaking.

Which is what Jack wished for, and got, in the end – freedom from the fame monster.

Subterranean Blues

after Jack Kerouac

"I say, I say fuck the monster"

How veil evil with the raped pared down
to drape the dead
the act been not so much
    matter of fact as
        manner of derangement for the
heart broke?

Look! The moon yowls pregnant with alley cat heat
hornèd gargoyles squat the tops of telephone poles
eaches piss their yellow reign
a familiar harried ape sneaks crêpe-footed
    across the flotsam & jetsam of history's slow decay
        to smoke tea in the back room of Dante's Bar
outside, death shrouds its feathery wings above the window
while Fame, that cracked goofball, shoots the glad eye
Mardou down, Beatrice further
& who seemed to love him hated him had no fellow feeling
one way or the other.

               Gone underground
purgatory held no desire
whereas heaven peered at the hole
haloed in hair that bristled straightaway to hell
his genitals alarmed even as the silver bullet
whistled his teeth.

Who wanted too much too badly
had it sewn inside the mouth
whether whorship of the primitive
mood of lyrical longing
cosmic sadness
or Buddha lost along the highway

made situationlessness
his gal.

Speak of the tremble, what was it kneed the shook
of those present afflicted & spooked in tongues?
Beat
Chinese
    or any other deep fried language
never the loneliest monk he went on the nod
unbuttoned his shirt
unzipped his prose
wailed: Bug, gimme my shadow!
Jug Jug, I dunt keer to wake.

O, if you see Kay, tell her I love her.

SØREN KIERKEGAARD

"So rancor kirks a card": playing again with the fractured homonym to introduce a new element into the poem – Fate and the Tarot – alongside Kierkegaard's own belief in blind leap of faith into the unknown; the mix of pagan superstition and Christian God and who's to know the difference until the final candle is doused?

I guess I'm just a sucker for stories and characters that suffer existential angst and contain a perverse bent for the melodramatic.

Either/Or

after Søren Kierkegaard

"Do it or don't do it – you will regret both"

How reconcile this slant line that hangs possessed as Lady Macbeth's dagger in the witchy air & augurs all pretty ones gone at one fell swoop? No ear honey poured into the porches either soothes the brain's darkest dreams or eases the heart's malcontent. Rather, a sharp tongue darts both sides of the mouth while a pair of horns twist the skull & bury themselves within the minister's bouffant fright wig. Oh, the horror, the horror! Seeming suspended somewhere between a rack & a hard peace, sore a'feared, trembled, sick unto death, who haggles the art of taking away the possibility of seduction cannot help but be seduced. Case in hand draws the tale of the Abraham/Isaac split where reverent daddy (pumped hard on with the voice of God) sets table, his most obedient son a capon trussed up for the kill, his fattened breast puffed toward heaven almost begging for the knife. Here resides sweet moment of truth set to escort singular man toward exit's angel. Yet, what shaky promise sudden has the cloth pulled out from under upon the signal of a bloody lamb's bleat – Jee-zus! – tangled amid the branches of a burning bush. All smoke earlier blown up the ass releases in a sulfurous blue cloud even as the golden gates slap shut & a melancholic Dane is caught with his pants down, *ad nauseam, ad infinitum*, neither Hamlet nor an attendant lord, another bit player among bit players. So rancor kirks a card from the fated deck: nine of swords, say, minor arcana (naturally), upright (of course), that roughly translates suffering, doubt, desolation, death of a loved one, suspicion. Go figure. Or Hanged Man, say, major arcana (again, naturally), feet kicking the air (again, of course, why not?), alive with its haloed wail of false prophecy & useless sacrifice that decrees its absolute: "If it be not now, yet it will come."

Yet it will come! Leap of faith be damned, when the abyss yawns & the arm drops, the single unholy ghastly lot will be the devil to pay.

KAREN MACCORMACK

I found much of Karen's collection of poems, *Straw Cupids*, totally confusing. I had no idea what many of the poems were going on about. At the same time, I enjoyed how they were assembled on some base level. I finally decided to let go of my strong attachment to 'meaning' and just allow the poems to 'speak' for themselves and affect me however they might, whether a word, a phrase or the construction of same.

re: placement

after Karen MacCormack

"between the two not a reference, this is the switch"

Omega isn't "Z" livid
abhor this worser facsimile
than impede refutation

ipse dixit
exempts it if
& all of nihil obstat outside
the languor

rob mclennan

rob is one of those rare people who is not only a prolific/talented writer/poet himself, he also reads, publishes and supports both younger and established poets with an enthusiasm and energy that is truly humbling and mind boggling.

How many times have I listened to him rave on about some poet or another he'd recently discovered and I'd have to say, sorry, I never heard of him or her, and rob would go, no? You have to, and hand me a fistful of the person's work or a chapbook he'd just put together, or a book, if he could afford it.

I don't think rob sleeps. In fact, I'm sure he doesn't.

I wrote this poem for rob as a thank you. Beyond that, he deserves a medal for the effort he puts in to promoting poetry in a climate that pays lip service to its artists, if that.

Red Earth, Black Moss

after rob mclennan

"tongue lasts longer than the skin"

borrowed, a borrowing
burrowed, a burrowing
a borough
a bureau
                    ~~of investigation~~
an act(ion) or place meant

say, where tongue stops & skin begins
say, between the legs
say, wet
say, wet between the legs

say, behind the ears

say: the most attractive thing
        a woman
        can wear
        behind her ears
        is

say, her ankles

or, (in)citing myself, say, the place
                        where
                        head over heels
                        becomes
                        heels over head

incites
is
in (sight) full

is
tongue
is
wet
        upon the red earth; the black moss

bpNichol

If you live in Toronto you can't hardly escape the ghost of bp and the influence he had/has on the writing scene. I first read his famous eight line poem carved into the pavement behind Coach House Press.

As a general rule, it's famous folk such as explorers or politicians who get a park named after them when they die – something peaceful, alive and fragrant – whereas poets are lucky to be remembered at all. In another poem I mused: "Perhaps a parking lot will be dedicated flat & orderly / bathed 24 hrs. a day in adoring, buzzy fluorescent."

Perhaps a lane. *Buzz*.

Forwards

after bpNichol

"a / lake / a / lane / a / line / a / lone"

four
words
for
lines

ANAÏS NIN

Difficult if not impossible to separate fact from fiction here, especially given that Anaïs Nin is best known and remembered for her explicit diaries. Oh, there are those few books of erotica she wrote for a gentleman who offered her hard cash for each story, but they're regarded as pretty tame fare these days.

It was the novel, *A Spy In The House of Love,* that intrigued me. The notion that one can't escape their own conscience; that it dogs you without half trying; waits patiently for you to crumble. Reminiscent of Raskolnikov in Dostoevsky's *Crime and Punishment*.

Yet, in her diaries she explains how – almost effortlessly and with complete confidence and *joie de vivre* (ah, the French!) – she is able to create elaborate lies in order to keep her various lovers from uncovering her sexual dalliances.

Remarkable.

Delta Of Venus

after Anaïs Nin

"Wherever I am, I am in many pieces"

Cheap psychoanalysis ought to rank aspirations to Orpheus torn limb from limb by the hoi polloi for acts of sexual indiscrimination, the parts floated down river with nothing but the music to melt a body whole. Saxophone maybe; maybe horn, the entire jazzed scene took hook, line, & liar within the hot Parisienne light. Beyond the normal incest, father to daughter, more PT Barnum than Freudian, a sideshow of severed flesh revealed beneath the slip, damp & harried, meaning (& unlike so many other *femme fatales* sawn & parcelled off indiscriminate by the governing mail) she carved herself & these pieces sat up & wrote. Several entered for a share. In rooms they came & went, went & came, no talk of Michelangelo, just the deal of lurid tale after tale over wine & butt ends of cigarettes. Hugo accepted a hand, Durrell a foot, Agee compromised any ass in a storm & did his awkward best to put the screws to. Roared longing Henry, "It is, after all, her! Even more delightful" despite the threaded cat gut, the scar tissue, the *chinoiserie* he knelt at the delta & taught his American tongue to French. Known for perverted tendencies (she believed everything she read, especially her own press), she dispatched letter after letter. The mass were initial underwhelmed. Rumour aroused that June bugs performed a *belle danse* upon one small pale breast & that a *ménage à trois* excited a nipple to leap & roll across the floor. A knee's sin bent *con à coq* amid the throes. A pair of slim ankles caught various eyes in & about several locations. That had them whistling, sure. Beatific in her detachment;

almost angelic, at end, a spy in love's house made confession her recorder. Little birds sprouted her shoulder blades with fantastic wings, made a flap, snatched her entire worked body far above the maddened crowd.

ARTHUR RIMBAUD

The first time I laid eyes on a sample of Rimbaud's poetry it had been translated by a Brit and I thought, what's the big deal? I put him aside for a few years, then went back as his name and reputation kept re-surfacing in my literary life. This time I chose a German translator, a person who'd decided to "live in Rimbaud's shoes" for awhile in order to do justice to the work. He didn't last long in that world. Said it would have killed him. I believe it. The booze and drugs alone, never mind the poverty and filth. Realize that Rimbaud was only eighteen at the time of his most recognized works; young, mad and indestructible.

Instead, the man opted to rely on his own skills as a poet and the big "as if …"

It was a wise choice that made a huge difference in my appreciation of Rimbaud and his work. It also made clear why some folk say that the term "translate" literally means "to destroy" especially if placed in the wrong hands.

Desolation Angels

after Arthur Rimbaud

"I became a fabulous opera"
> *Chapter Infernal: They rape my heart with what
> they say.*

Pagliacci being most obvious takes it up the ass *de rigueur*
amid the more palatable soap & horse persuasion, tears of a
clown appearing maudlin pathetic almost grotesque apace this
expansive bare stage whereas a drop of glycerine squeezed
from an ersatz idol's eye excites a long-faced audience glued a
lifetime to the square tube, an area so tightly proscribed that
few dare venture outside the plush velvet curtains never mind
attempt to dance on the tits of the forbidden for any no-good
goddamn reason, a spot where art hurt & rhyme bowed beneath
the weight of those pricked painted vowels, A E I O U, ah, oh,
ow, sweet enema bags of ecstasy! riot of piss yellow, vomit
green, snot grey, blood red, shit-brindle brown, that sometime
pale Y a black-faced crutch hobbled in from Africa sporting tight
stockings & spiky hair, foment of cancer sewn behind angelic
lips prepped as ever for the skirl of unbuttoned punctuation
even as the fairies chirp in with their *dont act effeminate, pal,
its unbecoming* soft-shoe routine, go figure … if there was no
Rimbaud, we would invent one, three headed, twelve toed,
slightly mad unholy ghostly, circumference everywhere, centre
nowhere, what is so-called human nature: to create that which
is not, then deny it, cock hung between legs crowing such
sad music; such sadness unlistened to, all vagrant prayers &
messages ended desolate in the dead letter box, I mean, how
waltz with a man clapped in electric body armour? how sing?
how jack each other off when a taste for blood is replaced by

a fetish for hand-carved shells & shoehorns? excuse my rut, my rant, but, no season in hell affords such luxury & no word-sperm of poems populated by strange stranger well-built young men makes more lasting than eighteen with a bullet, take a boo – sun weeps rose & all tigerish things mope lonesome as a cloud across the sawdusty star-struck boards wailing visions mordant as honey ladled from the mouths of exquisite corpses.

ANNE SEXTON

I've already written a short novel (unpublished, natch) using a character based on (parts of) the life of Anne Sexton: tragic, lost and suicidal. Anne's total short life was much too fictitious-sounding on its own to try and put into a single novel.

My favourite poems of hers are from her collection, *Transformations*, where she sets herself the task of re-visioning Grimm's fairytales: macabre, sexual, angry, violent and funny as hell in places.

She often performed her poems with a band called *Her Kind*. Just add alcohol and stir.

Her Kind

after Anne Sexton

"Rats live on no evil star"

It is precisely here she configures the baby with the bathwater.
Tossed upon this further storm-tossed shore. & so it goes.
Or so it went. Not half well. Not nearly, as, close to hand
    remains
        bones of a small animal rinsed clean.
The resemblance is worth remarking.
On & on & on the path is treacherous. But to stop?
Impossible. Doors open to her always.
One must be thankful for small miracles.
Kyrie eleison. Christe eleison. Kyrie eleison.
Do angels kiss she wonders?
Does one miss what one never had?
Often.
The dull *fffutt* of mud under heel.
Ah, the beauty of it all!
(she repeats seven times as in a trance)
Ah, the beauty!
Ah!
Still with hope the magic works here as well. Even here.
Among bones devoid of any sexual apparatus.
Among bones devoid of any obvious charms.
Among bones devoid of any lingered impression
                        beyond the skull's manic grin
Dug gravely by the sexton's hand & rudely deposited.
Alas, poor Yorick!
Still, one false move & it's up the stump, doll face.
Beside the bones; floating. Head above water, barely.

Mum's the word & whatever else improper enchantment
Meant to cage a drugged body in the high brick tower.
> *If that mockingbird don't sing ...*
Step on a crack? Yeah, fat chance.
Hair grows out of proportion in this childhood setting.
Tumbles out windows made fit
   for the climb of eaches rumpled daddykins.
Look! Eyes pop wide as saucers at the first wet bullfrog kiss.
Lips part & legs flop open as if the most automatic.
Every morning she brushes ashes from eyelids,
   raises hands to the light, peers through cigarette paper skin,
      studies the stretch & flex of her favoured slippering joints.
No matter what activity the hands remain. The hands. Remain.
The hands remain
What?
Tangled
   amid the hoodooed spin of straw to gold.
Tangled (as well) with desire to wash blood from the babe in
the cradle.
Thrill the tiny soul soared toward heaven.

> O, here's to the wound that never heals.
> The more you rub it the better it feels.
> Gentlemen, the Queen!

Ah, the beauty!
Ah!
Somewhere in the scape, the scrape of angel kisses.
Somewhere on the tongue the sweet lick of gingerbread.
Quick! Step on a crack!
As if. One false move
            & it's hands chopped twice at the wrists.
Mum's the word even as the tongue wags furious from its hole.
Nowhere for a princess with a bent toward ecstasy.

Meanwhile (trapped hungered in the bone) angels cry for meat.
O, pity the poor pudenda! Crucified amid the flap.
Hung to dry ripe & naked as a swell of shame-faced grapes.
Easy pickings for either big bad wolves or wicked stepmothers.

> *If that mockingbird don't ...*

In her ears the constant suck of mud.
One false move & it's up shit creek without a palindrome
   (save what's writ on the grave stone weighed heavy overhead)
Mum's the word. Step on a crack. Right. Easier said than done.
I mean, how avoid the smother: moth-eaten lion fur & pasty
wings?
The tender flesh riddled. The legs cut out from under.
Four then two then three.
Followed by clack of teeth; grind of bone on bone.
Whereas nothing hangs between the legs of an angel.
No thing.
But, the resemblance?

> *If that mockingbird ...*

Meanwhile, a halo of bones girdles the hunter moon signalling
   a call for witches to remove heads from ovens & take to the
ether.
For familiars to go on the prowl: her peter, her puss, her boots.
For skeletal horses to gallop headlong across railroad ties.
Note the clippety-clop clammer of metal shoes to wood
   that shakes the ground & trees alive with twisty snakes.
Nearby the tortured river churns its watery shroud &
   along the moist bank baby's breath flowers the dark night
Cryptic.
Though, this is not *that* story, this is *this* story. The other.
Her kind.
Where, in dreams, angels eat her.

> *If that ...*

Look! The witches hike their skirts & finger their sex.
Ah, the beauty of it!

Ah!

One almost believes the old magic.

Those gentle hands spreading the legs.

Suck of mud for a decent bone.

Who can tell a hawk from a handsaw, herr doktor?

A hawk from a mockingbird?

Where mum's the word & little girls

                    gobble sleepyheads like Tic Tacs.

Step on a crack. Step definite on a crack.

Witness the living exchange faces with the dead & vice versa.

With an unsteady eye she upraises a martini. Begins to poem:

> "I dream if I fell into a well
> & looking up to get out
> no one comes to get me out"

The same old same old fairy tale featuring

                    the same old same old outcast.

Complexed suicides & simple fuck ups

Dwarfed

Unboned in the old bone yard.

      If ...

      If only ...

Lullaby

after Anne Sexton

Lay undercover of a lie
spooks:
> who sings the body electra
> anymore
> beside the complexed heart

meaning
whose childhood bed does not pose a soft skin
for those things that go bump & grind in the night?
Whose bedroom closet is not a dark hole crammed
with the rattle of loose-boned skeletons; is not a hideaway
jammed with the ejaculate of trembled voices
that lip synch the wrong lyric, ever?
"Rock-a-bye Baby" or some such innocent refrain
struck violent in the pitch.
Case in hand draws a blank beyond the usual
sad foreplay: beat of breasts, gnash of teats
made up (as they are)
ghostly
in a mother's yellowed wedding dress
madly fondling their uglies amid the spidery gloom.
Or, outside the window, the scratch it makes
enough to bend any so-called happy home
perverse.
Where ripped deeds can't ease the pain
nor eugenics a'kneel in prayer can't untangle the twisty thread
drives a maid hysterical.
Listen! Mourning breaks, it utter wails.
Quiet dreams erupt visions of snakes birthed between a scrawl
of legs.

Wind haunts the branches of stately elms
& what sticks is every manner of horror
whether shit to a shovel or dog to a bone
worries it
this rooted upstanding & tall
unleafed rough daddy, O,
barks.

WILLIAM SHAKESPEARE

Sure, I tried to ignore the big guy and was unable. Saved him to near the end at university (Chaucer being last, which is another story) as I couldn't figure how he (his work) could possibly live up to the hype. In other words, I was prepared to shoot holes in the flimsy fabric that described a text that no regular person either understood or cared to understand: "But screw your courage to the sticking-place."

What?

Fortunately, I had a female Jewish Professor from New York (the Bronx!) with a penchant for Freudian analysis and a sense of broad humour who managed to make Shakespeare not only approachable but downright contemporary. And intelligent and sexy and funny and "human all too human."

And, yeah, another (further) existentialist.

Sonnet 116

after William Shakespeare

"Love's not Time's fool"

If a couple's of a true marryin' mind
Don't paint me the thorny prick. Love ain't love
That changes *presto* with nine-to-five grind,
Or splits at the first sniff of a new groove.
No way! It should be Rock of Gibraltar
That calms waves & never fucking flinches.
It should be gold standard for embarkers.
That thing you can't price in fame or riches.
Love should be forever though you are not.
Time flies & no nip & tuck can save ya.
Love springs ever while you grow old & rot,
Stomps your grave as you push up petunias.
That's my story & I say: so be it,
Prove *should* from *is* then all my love's been shit.

Enter Two Clowns

after William Shakespeare

"There is nothing either good or bad
but thinking makes it so"

O, otherwise everything was hunky dory.
Who never dreamt to tessellate a wasteland with human skulls
             or charge artless brains with murderous design,
rather
Takes a pull from the jug. Whistles.
HURRY UP PLEASE IT'S TIME
Whether in or out of joint
Bones a maiden's head senseless. Corpses a crowd in the violet
light.
Knows what grows larger the more one takes away
Is a hole.
Knows (as well) what *who-man-been* builds stronger
Than a mason, shipwright or carpenter
Is a grave
Maker
Indeed
Fool hardy
Connects nothing with nothing in the free for all
Ash to ash, dust to dust that amounts barely enuf to plug a beer
barrel
Or unable to play the beast with two backs any longer
With pranks & jibes (still)
             will aim to shake spirits from the cold ground.
Broke earth broke loose in the broke wind.

Whose sexton's shovel wholly undertaken navigates this
shallow plot
 [a man dressed as a woman dressed as a man]
Sures to its extant demise
As through the wormhole breeds spooks stared out from
eyeless sockets
Become a faint constellation coiled somewhere between Leo
& Hydra.
Tells us. Yells it. Sings
 the body's electric underground
Cardinal humours:

> Blood
> Phlegm
> Choler
> Melancholy

Fools
No thought worth the whistle.
So elegant
So intelligent
'Jug Jug' to dirty ears.

SAM SHEPARD

Again, at SFU, I thought it would be good if I took a theatre class in order to help me read my poems aloud in front of an audience. Also, I was recently divorced and thought I might get laid.

Beyond these practicalities, in my bowling alley days, I had gone to a fortune teller (recommended by my mother) who told me I should remain in the business world if I wanted to succeed, it would be simpler as I had a bent for it, BUT, if I was intent on a career in literature, I should become a playwright.

A playwright? Uncomfortable news for a guy who knew nothing about theatre, rarely attended theatre, had little interest in theatre, so … OK, what to do?

I ended with a minor in theatre and acted in several of Sam's shorter plays where I felt right at home in his seeming strange *American Gothic* sensibility.

Sam, meanwhile, goes on to play the ghost of Hamlet's father with a decidedly American cowboy drawl.

Escape

after Sam Shepard

A young man, maybe 19 or 20, sits on a chair behind a small round pub table. He drinks from a beer glass. He's a bit drunk, as if he's been there a while. He wears ragged blue jeans, a black T-shirt, a ball cap turned backwards on his head and worn sneakers. He speaks to the audience.

I know what you mean. I do. You finally reach your limit. You've had it up to here (*holds his hand to his throat*). You're chokin'. You can't stand it anymore. You're fed up. You get to that point where you simply wanna pack up and leave; say *screw it* to the entire shootin' match and haul ass outta Dodge. I've been there, believe me. I have. I mean, what good is anything if it doesn't make you happy, right? I mean, really, like, what? No good, that's what. No goddamn good at all. You might as well be hooked up to a fuckin' corpse draggin' it around. (*He drinks.*) You wanna know what my dream is? My escape dream? Notice I don't say *plan*, like it's ever goin' to happen, but ... anyway. It's pretty typical, I guess, pretty macho-male. No surprise there I guess, eh? But, there you go, I never claimed to be original or anythin'. My dream? Easy. Jump into a big old beater of a car, Buick or something. Yeah, Buick. Sixty-nine Buick LeSabre convertible, that's it. Uh, dented fenders, slashed rag top, cracked windshield, busted side view mirrors, dirty scratched white walls all 'round, body rustin' out, paint peelin', suspension shot. Whatever. That's OK. 280 horse power 350 four-barrel V8 3-speed automatic. Nice. A fucking gas guzzler; a tank. (*He stretches out in the chair, slides his feet forward under the table and places his hands like they're on a steering wheel.*) I jump in, slap her in gear and hit the accelerator. Va-voom! That's it. Simple.

Sit back and let 'er rip. I'm drivin'. Doesn't matter where. Who cares? I don't give a shit. Not along the freeway though, not unless I have to. Back roads mainly. Highway 2 around the lake, that sort of thing; rivers, woods, mountains, y'know? Through the small towns. Port Hope, Brighton, Cobourg, Trenton ... whatever ... the heartland; the fuckin' life-blood of the country. Fuck the cities! Know what I'm sayin'? Cities kill. They kill the spirit. They're death. You know that. Anyway, there's a radio in the car. That's it. No CD player or tape deck. No fucking iPod. Just a piece of monkey shit radio with a snapped antenna. Only picks up AM. One of the speakers has a loose connection so everything squawks. (*Makes squawking sounds.*) I turn it on and try to tune in all the Country Western stations along the way. (*Continues with the sounds.*) I keep punchin' buttons and twistin' dials until somethin' comes in. (*Still with the sounds.*) Maybe the music lasts an hour or more, maybe not. Maybe it only lasts a couple of songs or one song or part of a song with the signal jumpin' and fadin'. (*Squawks.*) It's OK. It's cool. Doesn't matter. I keep drivin' and searchin' out stations. That's the thing. The only thing. That's all there is. That's all I want. I don't stop for nothin' except gas, food, booze, the john and sleep. And no motels for me, no fucking way. I sleep in the car. Front or back seat. Plenty of room either way. Otherwise I'm drivin'. Got the pedal to the metal. The scenery whips by, it's all a blur; the tunes are cranked. (*He sings snatches of songs.*) "Guitars, Cadillacs and Hillbilly music ... Don't break my heart, my achy breaky heart ... I've got friends in low places ... You picked a fine time to leave me Lucille ... Car wheels on a gravel road..." Yeah, I've got a can of warm beer tucked between my legs and a warm six-pack sittin' at my feet. Fuck the cops; fuck everyone! You think I give a shit? I don't. Why should I? So long as I'm drivin' and the tunes are rockin', nothin', no one can touch me. I'm invisible. I'm the fuckin' breeze. (*He drinks.*) Sooner or later, the money goes – bye, bye – the credit cards are maxed out.

So what? I start stealin' what I need. I knock off gas stations, corner grocers, liquor stores, whatever. I shove a hand in my jacket pocket, point a finger, say stick 'em up pal and no funny business or I'll blast your fuckin' brains against the wall. Just like in the movies. Now, empty the cash drawer. While you're at it, gimme a bottle of Jack, a couple of tall boys and bag of Cheetos. I am a piece of work; I am one nasty hombre motherfucker. (*He laughs, drinks.*) I don't wash anymore, I don't take a bath, I don't use the toilet. That's all behind me. That's a whole other life. I toss my wallet out the window. I piss on the side of the road. I crap in farmers' fields and wipe my ass with a maple leaf. Time passes. More time. I don't know how long. Months maybe, maybe years. I head north, drive through Smith Falls, Bancroft, North Bay, Cobalt, Blind River. The gas tank reads empty but the old gal keeps goin'. Don't ask me how or why, she just does. I don't feel hungry anymore so I don't eat. I don't need to piss or shit or sleep or anything. I only need to drive and play the radio. I'm like a character out of a Kafka story. The names of the towns become more foreign sounding – Kapuskasing, Moosonee, Longlac, Nipigon, Pukaswa, Oda. Finally, the names become unpronounceable; the signs unreadable. I have no idea. Not a clue. I just drive and drive and drive because I've forgotten about the world and the world's forgotten about me. (*He circles his finger in a beer puddle on the table. He looks across the room as if spotting someone. He licks his lips.*) You could ride along with me. We could make love in the front seat of that beat up old Buick doin' a hundred-plus clicks an hour down the steep side of some winding mountain, you straddlin' me naked, screamin' and moanin', your tits bouncin', the radio blastin', the windshield blind with dirt and grime and the bodies of squashed bugs, the car leanin', the tires squealin', barely able to keep from slippin' over the edge and crashin' in flames on the rocks below. Meanwhile, you're ridin' me to the rhythm of Dwight, Lucinda, Emmylou ... We're both wet. We're soakin'. Yeah, baby. Oh, yeah. Our come floods the seat. Hell, it floods the whole goddamn car. We're swimmin' in it. We're up to our necks. You and me. Flyin' down the mountainside. Fucking ourselves to death. Fucking ourselves to immortality.

He eases back in his chair and stretches out, exhausted. Lights fade to black.

JACK SPICER

I had been writing poetry for a short time (influenced of course by other poets) and I can honestly say that it was Jack's *Collected Books* that affected a major shift in my approach towards what a poem could do or become. Not simply his poems, but his discussion of poetry within the book, especially his "conversations" with the dead Federico García Lorca and his "fake" translations: "When I translate one of your poems and I come across words I do not understand, I always guess at their meanings. I am inevitably right."

Unapologetic and fearless. He understood that it wasn't up to the poet to provide all meaning, all emotion, there had to be room for the reader to step in, muck around a bit and create their own path through the poem, regardless of what the poor poet may have intended and that was OK. In fact, it was best.

"A poet is a time mechanic not an embalmer."

Another poet I read and re-read, always discovering something new; always realizing that the dead continue to haunt and speak.

Alias

after Jack Spicer

> "Do anything
> But be a free fucking agent"

Or a postman.
Rilke's hot wet dream & why not? Nothing
    but ocean out beyond us & beyond that, further
    unspunked ocean.
Given charge over the dead letter box & its eaches
Slack-jawed mu-zak. Rimbaud or Kerouac, say,
    buggered up in Africa for price of a stamp. All that
    murky water
Crossing.
Surrealism being a cat of many collars sinks beneath the surf.
For all its melted watches & such.
For all its moustachioed Mona Lisas & such.
For all its flying lips & flaming giraffes & such.
Ends as an elevator blown straight to the gallows. Meanwhile
    walls riddle with ghostly Polaroids labelled AKA alongside
    a string of dubious achievements:
Theft
Rape
Murder
Quackery
Introduction of the criminal element that recognizes
    the fucking horror of being a writer in America. Whether
    cock in the mouth or tampering correspondence
    does not cut it
    does not pass GO, does not collect the necessary
    two hundred bucks.

Young Werther, also AKA, hardly bears resemblance
Hung as he is by the sentence.
A strange bird on a stranger wire
Spooked
Impossible for any kind
Wander.

Seppuku

after Jack Spicer

"I repeat – the perfect poem has an infinitely small
vocabulary"

Alone with words isn't anything
I would wish
Alongside a mouth choked with dried flowers
Or the ears with arsenic
Ah, the horror!
Witness
The leaf's serrated edge
Causally
Slit
      the moon's ripe throat
Hear death's rattle
Escape the gash
How
Who
What is it? Where?
Why
   does it number so few feet
& hair
All my darling pretty ones
All my

LUCINDA WILLIAMS

A buddy of mine gave me a CD of *Car Wheels On A Gravel Road* for a birthday gift. After listening to it, I was hooked. A voice full of pathos and whiskeyed sexuality, she puts a hard twist on Country Western music, infusing it with Blues, Bluegrass, Pop, Rock & Roll … even rap, and makes it work as her own.

My first impulse was to write a song rather than a poem for Lucinda. Thankfully, I realized quickly that this was not a good idea. I wanted to create a tribute to her, not a parody and certainly not a challenge, as I am definitely not a songwriter.

Clearer heads prevailed, though I hope there is at least some kind music to be heard in this poem, whether C&W or otherwise.

Ballad Of The Hot Blood Blues

after Lucinda Williams

"Now he drives the bottle deep into the night"

Difficult near impossible to have it both ways, love.
Whether longed for virgin whore or drunken angel
Prepares the bed linens for tears.
Rose, say, or Bird, flush with southern comfort
Ended strung out on a wire.
Miles down the line blown three sheets to the reedy wind.
Trane enters the verse merely as a black ghost among white
tracks
Love supreme (or some such) being an other lost
Romantic notion destined for wreckage in that ill-fated tunnel.
Love itself aches to be unbuttoned & (in the throes) is a total
different
Kettle. All is bliss. No pot to point an accusatory
Finger where alcohol oils the machinery's sweet side.

Convulsed, confused with love drives it to our gal
Harder (maybe) not.
Just this side of heroine herself (nonetheless) still kicks up a
storm
Hot & blue amid the heartbreak.
Still peels beer labels with a cracked nail.
Still gets her panties in a damp knot.
Still gets her nipples in a twist.
Who recalls headier days slipt gradual as a tongue between the
legs
Or belly licked by the crawl of a Gibson, anyways, remains
Bent to the bent lyric

Bleeding fingers & broken guitar strings

Canaries: What doesn't kill us makes us stronger is
A lie.
Croons: It cripples; makes walking wounded of us all.
As bloodied hearts spike to sleeves in that same awkward
fashion
& (I mean)
        road to hell paved, etcetera, with shredded tires & busted
glass
How often can the word mention, love, before it dims?
Drunken angel drives it
Never.

WILLIAM CARLOS WILLIAMS

The doctor is in. The doctor is definitely in.

What Williams' work has always exemplified for me (beyond *Paterson*) is the power of the short poem, and I know that I will never be able to shake the vision of a 'red wheelbarrow' or 'white chickens' from my mind, ever. These images are that clear.

Which is why I thought it only fitting to play with his short poem a bit and see what might develop.

I could go on. Maybe I will. Later.

1. The Red Wheelbarrow: *Re(Vision)*

after William Carlos Williams

so much ... ~~circles~~ ...
so much ... ~~orbits~~ ...
so much ... ~~sways~~
so much ... ~~rides~~
so much ... ~~connects~~ ...
so much ... ~~comprises~~ ...
so much ... ~~involves~~ ...
so much ... ~~includes~~ ...
so much ... ~~contains~~ ...
so much ... ~~configures~~ ...

configures? ... no ... definitely not ... a bit too ...

so much ... ~~qualifies~~ ...
so much ... ~~hinges~~ ...
so much ... ~~necessitates~~ ...
so much ... ~~assures~~ ...
so much ... ~~hangs~~ ...
so much ... ~~concludes~~ ...
so much ... ~~clinches~~ ...
so much ... ~~dictates~~ ...
so much ... ~~relies~~ ...

hm ... *relies* ... not bad ...

so much ... ~~determines~~ ...
so much ... ~~decides~~ ...
so much ... *depends* ...

depends? ... yes ... depends ...

so much depends ... ~~over~~ ...
so much depends ... ~~about~~ ...
so much depends ... ~~as to~~ ...
so much depends ... ~~among~~ ...
so much depends ...

what?

2. The Red Wheelbarrow: *redux canadiana*

"To make a start,
out of particulars
and make them general"

some such flounders
beneath

a colourless uni
vehicle

gloomed with spill
age

apart the fouled
poultry

3. The Red Wheelbarrow: *coda*

"No ideas but in things"

ok
though
enuf time spent, perhaps,
on this goddamned wheelbarrow
for all its intrinsic red
harmony
as devotion to:
       petals on wet black boughs
       pairs of ragged claws or
       blackbirds dissected 13 ways to
Sunday
looses its hold of a sudden
wails its sorry ass to St. Evens
& further holy ghostlies

       the twelve apostrophes, say,

that row of cardboard chickens
haloed white amid a glaze of rain
water
       (beware adjectives they bleed nouns)
if only we weren't so sore afeared
to choir beyond
these apparitions
whether
superstitious triskaidekaphobia
or brain damaged agnosia their
thinginess
proves unrecognizable

amid the hunt & peck
the scratch & score
in which any doctor might operate
        (insist always on the verb)
raw as pounded flesh
& whose fragmentary strain
might tessellate cathedral floors
with eaches
scuttled
    comings & goings

                Jug, jug

and what I want to know is
how do you like your blueeyed boy
Mister Death
               – e.e. cummings

Acknowledgements

Separate poems have appeared in the following magazines: *Rampike*, *Front Range* (US), *The New Quarterly*, *Dusie*, *The Fiddlehead*, *filling station*, *Peter F Yacht Club*, *NôD*, *Vallum*, *The University of Windsor Review*, *Sunshine* (UK).

Also the anthologies: *Rogue's Stimulus*, *Crave it!*, *Poet to Poet* and *Seek It: Artists and Poets Do Sleep*.

The poem "Henry's Lament" was nominated for the National Magazine Awards for poetry in 2011.

About The Author

Stan Rogal was born in Vancouver and has resided in Toronto for 25 years. His work has appeared in numerous magazines and anthologies in Canada, the US and Europe, some in translation. He has published 19 books, including 4 novels, 4 story and 11 poetry collections. He is also a produced playwright and artistic director of Bulletproof Theatre.

MARQUIS

Québec, Canada